DO YOU FEEL LOVED BY ME?

DO YOU FEEL LOVED BY ME?

Practical suggestions for more caring relationships

PHILIP ROGERS

1998

Do you feel loved by me?
Practical suggestions for more caring relationships

Published in England by
Living Well Publications, PO Box 980, Oxford OX2 0YB
Telephone 07050 074875 *(mobile phone rates)*

ISBN 0-9531380-1-1

Printed by The Guernsey Press
Cover and text design Will Shaman

Set in 11 on 14pt Monotype Plantin

The author and publisher would like to thank *The Independent* for permission to use copyright material.

ACKNOWLEDGEMENTS

I would like to thank the following people for their help in producing this book: my wife Jane, Kate Howlett, Alex and Seren Wildwood, Ann Hunter, Will Shaman and Donna Deeks.

CONTENTS

INTRODUCTION

This book is about loving relationships. I hope that it will provide inspiration for you in your relationships, and help you to be more of who you truly are, who you truly can be.

We seem not to expect, and to be ill-prepared for, positive, loving, supportive relationships. When I talk with people in groups and sessions, the idea that loving and supportive relationships are not only achievable but even a basic human right makes many people uncomfortable and seems to be disallowed for all sorts of reasons. The idea meets mostly with negative responses.

Right now you could say to yourself "I deserve a loving and supportive relationship", and see if you accept that fully and if it is actually happening in your life. Be honest with yourself. If your answer is less than a wholehearted "Yes" that you can see being made manifest in your life, then I hope what follows will help you to change this.

This book contains guidelines in the form of ideas and practical suggestions for you to try. They are derived from my experience over twenty-five years. These ideas work, they bring results. The people I have worked with have helped to create these ideas by their courage to explore themselves. I hope their gift can help to inspire you to put these suggestions into practice in your own life.

Where truth grows, love can flower.

DO YOU FEEL LOVED BY ME?

We put great emphasis on the words involved with love, and particularly the words "I love you". But why do we so rarely ask "Do you feel loved by me?"

It's sad to say, but it's not outside our experience, that someone may use the words "I love you" and it can be a lie, or can be said out of duty or habit. "I love you" can be arrogant, can even be used to claim something, as if in ownership. It can be conditional, meaning "I love you" therefore you must be like this or like that. It can be said expecting something in return like "I love you, too".

Many of us invest too much in wanting to hear the words "I love you". Yes, these words are important; we may feel loved when we hear them, but is that enough? The words of love need to be backed up by actions of love, by loving behaviour. If we listen too much to the words, we can fool ourselves into believing in a love that is there only in our fantasy, because of our need to feel loved.

So, the words "I love you" can be manipulative, but "Do you feel loved by me?" is a respectful question that demonstrates a positive interest, and can help engender a feeling of love between two people. It has much more of the quality of love. It's more open, like standing with your arms out. It's waiting for an answer rather than making a statement. When we change "I love you" round to "Do you feel loved by me?", this changes the whole nature of the communication.

What you are asking is not about your own feelings. You are asking about the other person and their experience. When you love someone isn't it more important that they are experiencing being loved rather than you feeling that you love them? You may be overflowing with love but if this is not reaching the other person, what then?

One of the qualities of love is a sense of expansion, an experience of expanding outwards and overflowing; where our boundaries are not so fixed, where we are more reachable, more permeable; where we are more able to connect and to relate to each other. But is this reaching the other person? Are they experiencing your love for them? You can find this out by asking "Do you feel loved by me?"

What's important is that you don't need to wait until you feel like that in order to ask. You don't need to feel this wonderful feeling of expansive love to ask the question "Do you feel loved by me?" Nor does the person you're communicating with; but in answering the question, they can talk about how they feel loved, and they can relate to their experience of being loved, and they can share it with you. This can be very helpful, because then you are talking honestly with each other and not relying on assumptions and mind-reading which can lead you into all sorts of trouble. We all know that it appears easier not to be so open and honest, to play games; but has this lack of directness helped you in your relationships?

People have said to me that it's frightening enough to say "I love you", and even more frightening to ask the question "Do you feel loved by me?" Yes, it does take courage. It's not necessarily easy but we need to know, and not make assumptions. If we are unwilling to ask or answer this question then that in itself is significant. We are allowing our fear to rule the relationship; and what is more important to you: fear or love?

The opposite of this wonderful feeling of expansion that we call love, is contraction, which is based on fear. People say that love and hate are opposites, but I don't think that's so. It is fear which says "Don't come close to me, don't touch me. I won't let you in, I'm not coming out, I need to defend myself." It is fear that gets in the way of asking and answering this question.

If we want a loving relationship with somebody to move forward, we need to pay attention to our fear, not our hate or anger. If you think about answering the question "Do you feel loved by me?" when it's being asked by somebody you care about, you can very easily sense fear and tension in yourself. This is OK, and not something to deny.

It's important to keep in mind in our relationships that it is this fear of intimacy, fear of closeness that mostly interferes with love, and that that fear needs to be respected. We don't invent it, it doesn't come from nowhere; it comes from the past and we don't need to carry it forever, but we do need to respect it in order to be free of it.

If we are willing to take the risk and ask this question,

what it leads to next is *how*. If the person replies "Yes", then we can say "That's good! How am I managing that? How is it working between us?" This is a wonderful communication to start to share – what it is, how it is, that we are loving. Even if the answer is "No, I don't feel loved by you", then this moves us in the direction of love, because this is the beginning of truth; and where truth grows, love can flower.

This respect for truth is demonstrating an intention to care for someone actively, and in a way that is respectful of their individuality. We can then base our relationship on this clearly demonstrated intention to be loving. Not in some perfect way, but in a way that is openly inviting the other to help us to love them. After all, we are in this together, aren't we? This is particularly helpful, because then we don't have to base our love just on feeling.

If we base our love relationships solely on feeling, we are basing them on ground that is going to change. One thing you can say about feelings is that they don't stay the same. This feeling that I've talked about – this feeling of love, this expanded state that so many songs are written about – is not going to stay there all the time. If you try to base relationships on a feeling that changes, then you're in deep trouble.

I would say that the intention to love is a better foundation: the intention to do the best you can to care for that person in the way that feels good to you, and also in the way that feels good to them. You are not imposing your ideas of love on them, though you may offer these ideas respectfully. When you have a conscious intention to love like this you are more open to being actually loving, rather than being stuck in a fantasy of love that can often be going on just in your own head. You are more able to respond to your partner and to get to know them. So if you ask them "Do you feel loved by me?" or "How do you feel loved by me?" then you can receive a response from them. They can tell you "I feel loved by you when you rub my back", for example. That's a pretty simple thing. You don't have to be in an expanded state of love to rub somebody's back. Of course if you are, then it's lovely; everything's wonderful when you're in that state, but you don't need to be in that place all the time to behave lovingly, and to be in a satisfying relationship.

"Do you feel loved by me?" is an intimate question to ask, and should only be asked very respectfully. You can't force someone to answer a question like that. Asked in the right spirit it encourages us to support each other in creating a loving relationship, and we do need to give our love support. There are many ways of doing this, having fun together, for example. Another way that I would like to suggest is reading together. Good books are very helpful. Finding inspiration in books has been an essential part of my own learning about love. When you read a book that is written from and about the heart you enter into that world, into that positive atmosphere. The wonderful thing about books is that you can choose when you read them, which means that you can choose to give your love support as and when you need it. Two books that I recommend are *The Art of Loving* by Erich Fromm and *The Prophet* by Kahlil Gibran. (See the resource section at the back of the book for more details.)

▶ EXERCISE 1

Giving and receiving love

This is a modern form of an ancient meditation attributed to Atisha, an enlightened master from centuries past. You can do it alone, or with a partner – try it both ways. It's very interesting to see what happens. It takes only a few minutes.

With a partner

First make sure you won't be disturbed for the allotted time. Sit facing your partner. Decide who will be active first, while the other is passive. The passive partner relaxes and closes their eyes. The other can either have eyes open or closed, as you choose. You might try it both ways and see how it is. As you breathe in, you breathe in the person opposite you. You take them into your heart as you breathe into your chest. You do that in whatever way has meaning for you. Your intention is to take them into your heart, to love them, as best you can. Then, as you breathe out, you send love to them from your heart. If you want, you can imagine a warm glow surrounding them as you breathe out. Do whatever brings you meaning to the giving of love, without any physical contact. Don't hurry the breath, don't slow it down either; let it be however it is. As you inhale, breathe them into your heart; as you exhale, send them love. After a minute or so, change over.

When you've both done it once, close your eyes and pause for a minute. Rest within yourself, see what's happening. Then do it a second time, without talking.

After the second round, after a quiet minute's pause,

open your eyes and look at each other and see if you have anything to say about it. Take a few minutes to talk with each other about it.

The next time you do it you can add a physical dimension to this by opening and closing your arms and chest when you are in the receptive role. As you breathe out let your arms and shoulders relax and as you breathe in let your chest rise and expand and your shoulders go back a little. Imagine that you are receiving love, being filled with it. As you fill your lungs with air, you are also filling your heart with love.

Alone

Imagine a particular person that you wish to send love to and follow the instructions above for the active partner. You could also imagine the whole world, or all of humanity; but begin by making it personal by choosing a particular person.

(There is an audiotape to accompany this exercise. Details are at the back of the book.)

Relationship happens when we are listening, and it ends when we don't listen.

CLEAN LISTENING

One of the main features of a good relationship is listening. There's no point in asking "Do you feel loved by me?", if you are unwilling to listen to the answer. It is quite an extraordinary experience, just to sit and listen.

Relationship happens when we are listening, and it ends when we don't listen.

I want to present you with the image of an ideal relationship, where you have two people with the intention to love who are willing to do their best to relate to each other on an equal basis, and are also willing to listen to each other. There is often an imbalance in relationships, where one partner tends to listen more. This can be a power issue which needs to be addressed if you want to relate as equals. For example, in the military, you have an officer and a soldier, and the soldier's job is to listen and the officer's job is to tell him what to do. That's an unbalanced relationship – a power imbalance which is explicit and agreed and works well so long as each person accepts their role. Power imbalances in relationships between lovers or friends get in the way of love. It works fine so long as both people are happy, one with being ordered about, the other with doing the ordering. But when one or both are unhappy with this, disruption occurs, change takes place, and a different dynamic for the relationship has to be found.

One of the ways in which you can address power imbalances in the relationship is by agreeing to listen to each other in a structured, balanced way. This means the 'less strong' one will agree to listen even if they have feelings that may make it difficult – for example, they may be scared of being overwhelmed or persuaded by the 'stronger' one. The 'stronger' person will also agree to listen, to keep quiet, when they may wish to correct or interpret the other person, probably because they have equally strong feelings of fear, though perhaps with less awareness of them.

Here is an outline for an exercise called *clean listening*. This is designed to demonstrate the benefits of listening and talking equally. By experimenting with this you will find out a lot about yourself and your partner, not only from hearing each other, but also by seeing how it feels doing it in this structured way. As you get used to the structure you can widen your use of it, but be aware that it is not a good method to use when you are angry. When you agree to listen to each other you need to be respectful; it is not the place for the speaker to take advantage of the listener. To be insulting, for example, is abusing both the other and the structure. It may be important to say how you're feeling; but it's also important not to use a structure like this to pour your feelings out onto somebody. So, if you're in a very emotionally charged situation, try to have some sort of external release for yourself separate from this: that is, some way of expressing these feelings, releasing them, so that you're not pouring them all into this structure. This exercise is not designed for that; rather it's designed to enable both of you to move toward some kind of mutual respect, some kind of clarity. Too much overcharged feeling will destroy this. So, have some place where, on your own or with the help of another person, you can release the charge of those feelings. It may be just running around the block, it may be therapy of some kind, or a punch bag, it doesn't really matter. Just the fact that you are able to release these feelings rather than letting them spill over too much into the structure is good.

Use the time to explore issues that are important to you both, issues you both choose. Some topics that people have found useful are:

What is your image of a loving and supportive relationship?

How does it feel to be a man?

How does it feel to be a woman? (These two questions are very interesting when men and women answer *both* of them.)

What are some ways that you feel loved?

What were your parents' attitudes to love when you were growing up?

You can use these or your own questions to explore your ideas.

In *clean listening* one person speaks and the other listens for five minutes, and then you swap over. When you're the listener, you only listen. This means that you do your best not to show any signs of agreement or disagreement with the speaker, to appear neutral. This means no nodding of the head, or smiling, or other gestures that we normally make in conversation. You're simply there as a listening presence, not bringing in your own responses or advice. All these things may be going on inside you, but your intention is to be as free from any signs of what's going on internally as you can be. Don't go off in a dream, looking around the room or out of the window, keep your attention on the speaker. Keep a soft, present attention on them and their face. However, if you do daydream, don't berate yourself; when you notice it, just come back to listening.

This has a very profound effect in many ways, and one of them is because of the equality in which you both speak and listen for the same amount of time. This is absolutely essential for this technique to work, even if your time is up in the middle of a sentence. It helps to have an external timing device, which will beep or ring. What you create when you do this is a reduction of the power dynamics that often interfere with relationships. Also, by making an agreement and both keeping to it, you start to build trust and mutual respect.

When you're listening in this way, you might be surprised how difficult you find it. Many people go into this thinking they're quite good listeners, and most people discover this is not the case, that actually simply listening is very challenging. We can appear to be good listeners giving all the right responses and at the same time be occupied with the voices and judgements in our heads. All that you're asked to do in this technique is to give your partner your attention, doing your best to be present for that person.

When you first start listening in this way it is likely to feel unnatural. That's fine, that's part of the process. Let any thoughts come and go, don't resist them, or try to chase them away. Don't do anything with them. The thoughts are there, they come, they go, you just focus on listening to the speaker.

As with any new activity, you may meet with some kind of resistance at first that needs to be passed through, but as you pass through that you will find a place of relaxation. "I don't have to do anything. I can just listen?" What a relief! And you come to a very natural place inside yourself which feels deeply peaceful.

When that happens to you, something amazing can happen *between* the two of you. The speaker is drawn into speaking, and sometimes they don't know what they're going to say and then, in a strange sort of way, they begin to start listening to themselves. The rehearsing and the censoring we do with the mind when we're speaking starts to get undermined, and we start to move into new, unexplored or barely conscious areas of communication. This might take some time and practice, but I've used this technique with many people who reached this state.

As the speaker, you may feel abandoned. We mostly get a lot of feedback when we're speaking, even if it involves a lot of interruptions, but this *clean listening* is different: there are no interruptions and there's no-one giving you feedback (nonverbal or otherwise). Any uncomfortable feelings that arise are part of what needs to be gone through; stay with it and allow yourself to experience your feelings as fully as you can, talking about them if you choose.

Another point which makes it easier for the listener to hear what is being said (particularly if you are saying things about them) is to use the first person. By speaking with 'I' statements, for example, saying "I feel as though you're not really listening to me", rather than "No-one ever listens to me". Speaking about the *feeling* in you, rather than the thoughts or opinions you have about it, makes you much less likely to invite defensive statements back. Also, you are speaking more closely of the reality when you say how *you* feel.

The ideal is that you're speaking from your senses and your heart, not just from your intellect, where you've got all these things worked out and rehearsed, knowing what's coming next. Instead, I'm suggesting risking being in what can be a very vulnerable place of communication, where both people take it in turns to listen in a non-judgmental way.

This gives both people a tremendous freedom to speak, and you start to realise how you limit yourself, how much you censor and inhibit what you say to the other.

When you've tried this, you can go on to a further development of this technique. Sit down with your partner and agree to do this change-over three times, so that it lasts for a total of thirty minutes. When you do this, it's very difficult to know what you're going to say by the time you're in the third five minutes. What may start to emerge is the more mysterious and the more unknown, which can be very enjoyable, and also rewarding and enlightening.

It can also be very helpful in a time of stress. For example, if there's some very difficult issue between you, sitting down and listening to each other can be a way through. There's a funny thing that has happened to me a number of times when doing this. I'll be listening – I'll be listening to my wife Jane in this case – and she'll say something when it's her turn to speak and I'll be incensed – "How dare she say that, that is so unfair!" or whatever. But I have to sit and be silent, because that's my role at that time. I have to wait until it's my turn, and then the five minutes ends and it's my turn to speak and I can't remember what I wanted to say. That has happened to me on a number of occasions. Two minutes before, it was so important to me; two minutes later I can't even remember what it was. This is one of the reasons why this *clean listening* structure can be very helpful when you're in a struggle. You can cut out all the reactions to the reactions, and actually get down to the more important issues that are going on.

I've used this technique where, over a series of sessions, we've extended the speaking and listening to forty minutes – one speaks for forty minutes and the other listens, and then you change over. The atmosphere in the room when this is happening is absolutely extraordinary, a sacred feeling. Something very precious is being exchanged. The speaker is giving, the listener is giving, and they are also both receiving. What is created gives all the people in the room a sense of something miraculous, a taste of the source of our being, which I would call love in its largest sense.

We've looked at listening and we've looked at speaking, and the third thing is "Am I being heard?"

There is a technique for this, too, called *mirroring*. What happens is that the speaker has their turn to communicate something, and the listener is there to do their best to listen and understand. The communicator, having spoken, then asks "What did you understand?" The listener will say what they understood, and at any point the speaker can say "Hold on a minute, that wasn't what I meant. This is what I meant." And so then they speak again. You continue this until the listener has given back to the speaker an understanding that the speaker is happy with. You then change over.

It's very important you keep it simple at the beginning. Don't try to communicate pages and pages of difficulties and issues, keep it simple and short, because the purpose is to know that you can be heard and understood, not to test the listener and then chastise them for mishearing.

When I teach *clean listening*, a worry that is often expressed is that five minutes is a long time. If five minutes seems too long, start with two and gradually build up. It's important not to make it an endurance test and it's important to stick with your agreement, so it's better not to make it too difficult.

Another concern often expressed is "Isn't it difficult to keep speaking?" My reply is "Try it". The vast majority of people end up feeling the opposite, they want more time. Remember, it's *your* time. You can say what you want, it's up to you. Make the most of it and enjoy it. We often enjoy things more if they're a bit scary!

▶ EXERCISE 2

Clean listening

Listener

When you're the listener, all you do is listen. You don't interrupt, you don't comment, you don't agree or disagree. The structure is that you just listen and then your partner will do the same for you. Do your best just to be present, listening.

Speaker

When you're the speaker, use the opportunity to talk honestly about what's important for you. It's your time, you can say or not say whatever you want, and your partner is agreeing just to listen. Use the time in the way that is best for you. I encourage you to talk about your feelings and try not to intellectualise. As you do this more you will find that you can't prepare what you're going to say and so you end up listening to yourself, as well as your partner!

Time boundaries

After you've done this once or twice, five minutes each, extend the number of times, first to two, and then three change-overs, so you end up doing it for a half hour, three times listening for five minutes and three times talking. At the end, don't discuss it immediately, give yourselves five minutes' quiet time before you talk about it together.

Benefits

When you do this structure, it's very important to keep the boundaries, because then you create equality, a balanced communication. Most couples have an imbalance in talking and listening, usually one does more talking, the other more listening. This structure evens this out.

Another reason for doing this, and keeping to the agreement carefully, is that it helps to build trust. This may sound too simplistic, but it's my observation that trust is easily damaged in poor communication between couples. Demonstrating that you can keep this agreement to listen to each other can begin to repair mistrust and imbalances of power, and to rebuild the trust that is essential to honest and intimate communication.

*Guilt is a form of anger
turned in on oneself.*

EMOTIONAL HONESTY

Honesty is central to any intimate relationship. This doesn't mean being perfect, it means having the intention to be as honest as you can. However, in order to do this, many people need to know more about their basic emotions. Intimacy needs to be rooted in a deep awareness of these emotions and time and again I have seen that it is with the so-called 'negative emotions' – fear, anger and pain – that people have the most difficulty.

There are complexes of emotions that you can sort out into fear, pain or anger, or combinations of the three. For example, jealousy is a combination of fear, anger and pain. Guilt is a form of anger turned in on oneself – "I'm a bad person because I did...". Loneliness is a form of pain, perhaps with fear too. It is very helpful to put clear names to our emotions and to separate them into these basic ones. When we don't do that, often we have a mixture of unidentified feelings that can be very confusing.

Many of us have been taught to ignore these emotions by those who took care of us. (This is not said to make those people wrong, in most cases they were doing their best as they saw it; but if they made mistakes then it is up to us to put these things right in our lives now.) If we've been shown and taught not to feel our emotions fully, when we get to adulthood we need to do some work in order to recapture and regain them in order to come back to the full, emotional beings that it is our potential to be. That is, emotional in a balanced way, not at the mercy of our feelings, or driven by them, but with an awareness of how important they are and of how much they tell us that is important to our living full and happy lives.

If in our past we've had to learn to repress fear, anger and pain, often now we have difficulty even recognizing them and separating them from each other. When we start to identify them, that can be the first step in having greater awareness of them and the effect they are having in our lives. Many people are unaware of what their emotions are at all; others get stuck in one emotion (for example, always crying whether it is appropriate or not). Others have an automatic anger or irritation as their first response. We have within us a wide range of emotion and this is priceless, particularly in our relationships, because it connects us to what is outside us. So the more we can feel these inner movements clearly, the more we can use them for their true purpose, which is to help us in our lives.

We start this by acknowledging them on a simple level, labelling them clearly – "I am feeling afraid now", or "I'm angry", or "I'm feeling hurt". To help this process here are some statements which are quite revealing. You can substitute the words *fear, pain* or *anger* in any one of these statements, whichever feels appropriate for you. Take some time to consider the following statements and see what they mean to you, what reactions and responses you have.

Within the pain I feel, there is something good for me.

The emotion of pain alerts me to something that I need to know.

And most difficult, perhaps,

Pain has a place in my life.

Mostly, we don't have any problem with this last statement on a physical level; when we bang our knee we accept we need to be more careful. However, there are people with a mysterious and, fortunately very rare illness, who don't feel physical pain, and these people have very challenging lives. Imagine the damage you would do to yourself if your leg was broken and you didn't feel it, and carried on walking on it. Physical pain is clearly helpful to us to prevent us damaging ourselves further. If we have repressed our emotions too much, then we will be in the same situation on an emotional level. If we deny we are feeling any emotional pain, that will very often lead us into all sorts of other difficulties.

It's exactly the same for the other emotions. "The emotion of fear alerts me to something that I need to know." That's not so difficult to imagine if we're in some kind of threatening situation – the information comes in, the emotion of fear is there, and it's telling us something we need to know.

It's not so easy for people in our culture, generally speaking, to believe that "The emotion of anger alerts me to something I need to know", but if you take that statement on, take it as something true (which I believe it is), then you begin to see that these emotions are there for our protection.

There's a purpose for every emotion in us. It's there in

us naturally. It's up to us to find out what that purpose is. I suggest that if we are cut off from the emotions of anger, pain or fear, then we don't have the protection that we need. We're liable to get ourselves into situations where we're not properly protecting ourselves. For example, there was an atmosphere of sexual freedom in the Western world after the Sixties, which led many people to jump into bed with comparative strangers, without listening to any 'inner voice' that might be suggesting they went more slowly, or questioning whether this was what they truly wanted. Many people can now look back and realise that what they actually wanted was a feeling of closeness, or affection, rather than sex purely for the sake of sex.

I think that many people in this kind of situation need to listen more carefully to what they are feeling, and to listen to the voices connected with their feelings that are saying "Wait, don't rush. What's the hurry?". When they don't listen, all too often it can become a painfully empty experience.

We need the information that comes from our emotions in order to take care of ourselves properly. We need to be in touch with our emotions, acknowledging them, listening to them, and being able to express them and communicate them when we choose. The connections that we create when we do this are satisfying and fulfilling on very ordinary, human levels. Being able simply to state what you are feeling in a way that can be heard and understood brings an ease to our lives and to our hearts.

To be able to do this we need to know our emotions. To feel pain fully, we need to be able to cry. This is nature's mechanism to help us both feel and release our pain. If you can't cry, you build up a great pressure within you of unfelt pain. You may have judgements about crying, for example "It's weak to cry." Many of us, particularly men, have absorbed this idea. However, very often the opposite is true, that it takes courage to cry, to feel our pain. It is a physical release, it comes through the body and that means letting go of thoughts and judgements in the mind that might stand in the way of the tears. Crying is healthy because it releases stress from the body – which is where our emotions are experienced, much more than in our minds.

When we are frightened, there are two quite opposite instinctual responses: *contraction*, an attempt to shrink and disappear, where the breathing constricts; and *fight or flight*, where the body suddenly becomes capable of great feats, of running fast, leaping out of the way, of striking out, of roaring or screaming. Afterwards, when the fear passes, whether you have frozen or leapt into action, your body will shake and tremble, if you allow it. All these responses are primarily physical – the mental or thinking part of you is secondary at these times.

We need to have these emotions in a proper balance and for some of us this means allowing an easier route for them so that they are available when we choose. We need the information that our emotions can provide; the thinking part of us is not enough on its own.

For some people, their emotions are too available; they come too quickly and too easily. Achieving some control over their feelings is just as important to these people as the need to lose some control is for others. These people need to bring the thinking part of themselves into their emotional situations more, in a constructive way. We all need to find a balance and the way to do this is through the body. Whether you need to let go more or to have more control you can start with the breathing and grounding exercise below. Using this you will begin the process of returning to a more balanced emotional life by being more fully in your body. This will help you to be more honest about your emotions in your relationships and give you more choices in how and what you communicate.

▶ EXERCISE 3

Breathing and grounding exercise

Begin by finding a space and time that is private, where you won't be disturbed for a few minutes. Stand with your feet slightly apart – the same width apart as the distance across your shoulders, and with your feet parallel. You'll find that there's a tendency for your feet to splay outwards; whenever you notice that, bring your feet back to parallel. Let your arms be loose, hanging by your sides, and take a couple of deep breaths right down into your belly, breathing in fully and exhaling fully.

Now flex your knees, pushing them back, and then letting them go forwards slightly, softening. Do that a couple of times until you get the sense of standing with your knees slightly softened, not rigid. Take a couple more deep breaths, fully in and out, staying aware at the same time of your knees being soft and your feet parallel.

Stand relaxed in this way and breathe down into your belly. Imagine that as you breathe into your belly you are breathing up through your feet from deep in the earth. You can imagine lines of force or energy coming up from deep in the earth like the roots of a tree, and that your legs are the trunk of the tree. You are breathing in energy through these roots, up into the trunk, through your legs, into your body. Every time you breathe in you fill yourself with energy from the ground; every time you breathe out, imagine that energy going out through the top of your head like the spreading branches and leaves of a tree, giving that energy out into the air.

Do this a few times, breathing the energy in through your feet and out through your head. Imagine yourself becoming more and more rooted in the earth as you do this.

If you need to be more aware of your emotions, as you breathe in this grounded way, bring your attention to your belly and ask yourself what emotions you can identify as you stand there. It may also be helpful to recall a recent situation where you were feeling emotional or under stress about something. See if you can experience some sense of that emotion in your body, and whether you can label it as either fear, pain or anger. If the thinking part of you is interfering, just go back to the breath and the grounding. You may need to do this a few times before you can feel the benefit.

If you wish to gain more control over your emotions, use the thinking part of you as you do the grounding to clearly identify and distinguish between the emotions of fear, anger and pain, and ask yourself what it is exactly that you are feeling angry or hurt about, or afraid of.

Come gently out of this exercise, knowing that you can take this grounded feeling more and more into all aspects of your life by being aware of your feet, which are always there.

Once you've got the hang of this exercise, it helps to stay within yourself if you do it with your eyes closed.

What am I not doing, that I could be doing, that I am blaming him/her for not doing for me?

THE POSITIVE EXPRESSION OF ANGER

In an intimate relationship that is honest we often get caught in worries about our anger, and that it will get in the way of loving each other. In fact, if you understand about the positive expression of anger, the opposite is true. Anger can support us in loving each other because it helps us to stand up for ourselves. The expression of anger that is generally seen is destructive, and that is not what I'm talking about. There is such a thing as positive, constructive expression of anger. Consider these statements:

Anger has a place in my life.

Allowing anger from the past to be felt releases me.

Within the anger I feel there is something good for me.

These statements are all true in my experience and if they are not true in your experience then you only know the negative expression of anger. A positive expression of anger, in its simplest form, is saying "I feel irritated", or

"I'm annoyed", or "I'm angry". It's not blaming any-body, it's just speaking of one's own emotion: "I feel angry." There's nothing wrong with *feeling* angry. It does no harm to anybody; it does nothing to any other person. The next step is where the difficulty comes in. How do I express my anger positively? If I feel angry I can *be* angry, I can stamp, I can shout, I can allow the emotion in me to have physical expression through my voice, and through my body. If no-one else is present, it's just "I feel angry". There's nothing wrong with this, it's not negative, it's not destructive – how can it be?

At this point many people start saying "Yes, but it's wrong to be angry", and I say "Think about it again. Anger is here in us, it is much better to find out its true purpose than to attempt to deny it or to make it wrong." Then we talk about the statements written above.

A helpful form of being angry I suggest to clients is using a bat – a nice big, toy baseball bat or tennis rac-quet. They make a very satisfying sound when you hit a cushion with them. If you use a bat to be angry, to be fully angry, to hit a cushion with, and use your voice to say "I'm angry", this is a positive expression of anger. It might be related to somebody else, you might be feeling angry with somebody, or some situation – that's fine. But they don't even have to be there in order for you to feel it, in order for you to express it. This is creative, this is expressive, it's positive, it's releasing. On the other hand, I'm sure you all know what happens inside you when you feel angry with someone and you don't do anything about it, for whatever reason: you go on thinking about it. You think: "Well, I could have done this, or I could have said that and if they'd said this, then I would've said that..."

And it can go on for days, or even for years. If you get a bat out and start whacking your bed or your sofa and saying the things that you're thinking and putting them out in your voice, you might feel very self-conscious, you might think "This is really silly", but you won't go on obsessing about it.

When we consider statements such as:

"Allowing anger from the past to be felt releases me", we're talking about a positive expression of anger, not something negative or destructive – like blaming, for example, "You did this to me, you're a bad person, you shouldn't do this, you're wrong." These kinds of angry statements are verbally abusive.

Or take hitting someone. This is physically abusive. Hitting someone when you are angry is a negative expression of anger, particularly if you are bigger than that person. Imagine if someone is angry, and they hit a child who's small and powerless. If you think about a four- or five-year-old child, about three feet tall, and you think about the size of the parent in relation to that child, they're like a giant. Think how big that person would be in relation to you now, where you're standing five or six feet in the air – they'd be bigger than the room. And this large person has tremendous power. All our myths about giants could come from this. We all lived with giants when we were growing up, and they were very, very powerful.

Unfortunately, many of them had no knowledge of what we're discussing, they didn't know about the positive expression of anger, and they were left to carry their anger and pain and they probably dealt with it badly. We're not here to crucify them or to blame them, but we *are* here to set it right. We set it right by getting it right in our own lives, and not passing it on. I feel this is particularly important in relation to anger. If the statements I began the chapter with take root in our lives and take root in the lives of our friends and our families, and more people start to think they are true, then our world will change.

When the Prime Minister of Israel was assassinated, the young man who killed him was reported to have said that God told him to do it. Well, I don't think God tells people to be violent. The young man was mistaken, in my opinion. I do know that he was very angry, this young man, and he didn't know anything about anger other than its destructive expression. I don't think you can kill somebody, shoot somebody, unless you're very angry. You may be deeply unconscious of it but it is that very repression that leads to the kind of dehumanising that makes such violence possible.

As I grew up, both at home and at school, I was told very straightforwardly "Don't be angry; that's not OK". I can remember my parents saying things like that to me, and they also modelled that in their behaviour. They rarely became angry themselves, and, if other people became angry, they were disapproving. So the message was very consistent as far as they were concerned. At school it was not consistent, I was told "It's wrong to be angry" by teachers who were often angry themselves. So, like most people, I hid my angry feelings away, even from myself.

It wasn't until I was in my mid-twenties, when I joined a therapy group, that I was introduced to the notion that anger could be expressed in a safe environment, that it wasn't something to hide, or suppress. By then it was actually very difficult for me even to acknowledge that I got angry at all. Apart from sarcasm, I didn't have access to anger in any way other than as an out-of-control explosion, and I was frightened by that and felt ashamed if it happened and so I avoided it as much as I possibly could.

Many people whom I meet and work with are in a similar position, and in our society at large I see the same messages as I was given being propagated all the time. This can be addressed on an individual basis, that is, in one-to-one relationships of all kinds, not least in the therapeutic relationship. It can also be addressed at a wider level, for example, in classes on anger management; but we really need a total re-education about the whole concept of anger. Learning to let anger out *in an appropriate way* from an early age would be a good beginning and much healthier than suppressing and denying it.

When we suppress anger it can easily become resentment. It burns away inside us and affects our behaviour, sometimes for the rest of our lives. Do you remember a time when you burned with resentment for days at a time? You can go on thinking obsessively about it in your mind. This energy runs amok inside us, particularly when we suppress it, and causes great destruction in our relationships.

Sulking and blaming is another way that suppressed anger is expressed negatively. The sulker slopes off, turns his or her back, and sulks – trying to make the other person feel bad. My own experience of sulking is that it's very miserable. There *can* be a sort of secret joy in it, you can fantasise about the other person feeling really sorry, and then begin to feel self-pitying and maybe self-righteous too. Blaming then comes into operation, because it is much harder to accept your responsibility in a situation than it is to blame the other person. There is a wonderful sentence that is very helpful when we are stuck in blaming:

What am I not doing, that I could be doing, that I am blaming him/her for not doing for me?

When you ask yourself this question honestly you are beginning to take responsibility for your situation. You are beginning to be able to respond to the situation rather than react. With this question you start to claim your own power instead of giving it away.

Another common inappropriate way of being angry is to stay silent. When somebody is being silent and not wanting to communicate, that's passive anger. For example, someone is upset and is not saying anything about it and their partner asks "What is wrong?" and they answer shortly "Nothing". In a devious way they have managed to let the other person know that they are angry. In fact, it's selling guilt to the other person, almost like saying: "I want you to feel bad because you did something to me." A more appropriate way of behaving might be to say: "I felt really hurt by what you did; I really hated it, I felt horrible." So the feeling is acknowledged. Refusing to communicate is very destructive.

Verbal abuse can also be a form of destructive anger. Do you remember that old verse "Sticks and stones may break my bones but names will never hurt me"? Well, it's not true. We *can* all be hurt emotionally by words. What is important is to learn how to express your anger in such a way that you minimise the amount of hurt caused.

And the first step in that is to acknowledge that the anger is there, that it exists.

If you acknowledge that, you also have to acknowledge that it has a right to exist, and that anger of itself is an emotion like any of the 'positive' ones that we often prefer to have. Anger then becomes something that is natural and consequently deserves its place in human beings.

It is up to us to find out what that place is and what anger consists of. If, like me, you weren't given much help in that respect when you were young, you may find that it helps to be around people who have learned to respect their anger in this way. You may find that you too will be able to consider that it's OK to be angry.

Actually being angry, both physically and verbally, is very energising. Initially, it can be difficult, it may feel very hard, and you may find a lot of resistance in your body as well as your mind. It was quite a revelation to me, after twenty-five years of life in my body being told that it's not OK to be angry, and then all of a sudden being actively encouraged to be angry! My body protested with its muscles, and my mind protested, saying "Don't do this, this is crazy; what will people think of me?" But when I overcame that initial resistance, the actual result of doing it was very liberating. I felt full of energy and life, and I understood that the purpose of anger in my life was so that I could stand up for myself. I could stand up and say "This is who I am". I was able to stand on my own two feet and say "No".

You see little toddlers doing this every day, very naturally. They literally stand their ground and they stamp, clench their fists and they say "No". Unfortunately, too often, at that point, Mummy or Daddy, or whoever, comes along, and says "Don't be cross", or something similar. Rather than validating the child's feelings, they manage to communicate the idea that being angry, *per se*, is bad. (This is not to say that the child must always get what it wants, but it is very important that the parent doesn't make the child *wrong* for being angry.) A better way is to let the child express feelings, to wait and not react.

If we don't have access to this vital energy of healthy anger then we can become very wishy-washy. In intimate relationships this leads to all sorts of difficulties. For example, if your partner doesn't do their share of the work around the house and you don't tell them that you are angry about it. Or, if your partner is often late and you say nothing because you are afraid of confrontation. If we are afraid to speak up we can become easy to manipulate, pushovers, easily moulded. This, of course, has great advantages for those who control our society. Wilhelm Reich wrote a book about this called *The Mass Psychology of Fascism*, where he went into this idea very deeply, considering the psychological benefits to a fascist society of having people who are manipulable, and who are scared of authority. They do what they're told, and they are suggestible. There are a lot of advantages to a hierarchical society like ours in having people that are easy to push around. So the anger work I am suggesting meets resistance from outside ourselves as well as from within.

Bioenergetics, a system of body therapy devised by a student of Wilhelm Reich, Alexander Lowen, is a specif- ically constructed and supportive way in which anger and other emotions can be safely and appropriately expressed. For example, it gives people the opportunity to 'have a tantrum' just as if they were a child again. There's an interesting fact here – every small child in every culture expresses deep frustration in basically the same way – by lying on their backs and drumming their feet on the ground. There are great differences in emotional expression between, say, Eastern and Western cultures, of course. (For example, Japanese people may have very strong inhibitions about the expression of anger, even more than we do, but nevertheless their children have the same 'tantrum reflex' – a built-in instinctive set of movements for the expression of anger.)

It wasn't easy for me – I was afraid during these bioenergetic exercises, and I remember thinking that I'd kill somebody. I was afraid that within me there was some kind of murderous rage that was strong enough to kill someone if I went over the top. Many people, I think, have that fear, and it's not so unreal. I'm 6'1" and I weigh about thirteen stone, and if I really hit somebody, it would hurt them. What I discovered, however, was that if I work with this energy, and if I release it in appropriate ways, it doesn't hurt anyone, neither me nor anyone else. We can learn to know the limits of our anger, and so stop being afraid of it.

In practising being angry you are more likely to actually become angry. It might begin as an act, but this enables you to get in touch with the real anger that is inside. I had a lot of repressed anger in me, and as I practised these exercises, I contacted it – twenty-five years of previous anger with my mother, my father, my sister, my brother, the teacher from school, or whoever. It was anger about things that I had the right to be angry about, things that happened to me in the past when I couldn't stand up for myself because I was too small and my right to my anger had been denied. I needed to feel and express this.

I didn't end up with no anger at all – I now have the ability to be angry when I choose. I didn't have that choice twenty-five years ago. If somebody pushed my boundaries I could turn the other cheek, but it was just pretending. I was walking on fragile ground, rather than holding a solid position. So, for me, being able to stand my ground doesn't mean that I have to go around being aggressive everywhere. What it means is that I have the ability to stand my ground when I choose, and when I think it's appropriate. This has had an enormously beneficial effect on my relationships.

Most of the time, in fact, it's not necessary to get angry. My experience is that when you have the choice of a full range of expressions of anger, an inner strength is somehow communicated which is felt and respected by the other person and what we think of as angry confrontations actually happen less and less.

▶ EXERCISE 4

Cushion bashing

Alone

Create a private space for yourself where you can make as much noise as you want. It may be helpful to put on some loud music so that you are less self-conscious. Take a tennis racquet or something similar and hit a big cushion, or the bed, or the sofa. Raise the bat over your head and hit with your full force. It makes a very satisfying sound! Do this a few times to get the feel of it. Now include your voice. As you hit say "I'm angry." It doesn't matter if you feel it or not, at the beginning act as if you are. Keep hitting, do it ten times, each time you hit saying "I'm angry" more and more loudly until you are shouting as loudly as you can. At the same time make each blow of the bat harder and harder until you are hitting and shouting at the tenth blow with all your might.

Once you've got the feel of this, take the bat and just be angry with it for two minutes, without the building-up process. Just hit freely and shout with all your energy. Say whatever comes into your head. Don't censor it. If you get stuck with words, try "No", or go back to "I'm angry", or just scream, make a noise, let any wild sound come out. Then sit back and close your eyes and rest, see what is happening inside you.

Try doing this every day for two weeks for at least two minutes. Let the time get longer if you want.

With a partner

Start off doing this side by side. Repeat the process described above, only hitting alternately. This is not a competition, use each other's energy to help you escalate your expression. Next you can try doing it facing each other. When you do it for two minutes, one of you uses the word "No" and the other "Yes". Don't listen to the other, just get into the energy of the word as it is coming up in you at that moment. Then change over, the one saying "No" now uses "Yes" and vice versa. Then sit back and close your eyes and rest, see what is happening inside you.

Afterwards talk about it a little and congratulate each other on your willingness to take risks!

Now it's time to close your eyes
and stay alert!

GOING WITHIN

When we do these exercises in a workshop I give people time to integrate what's been happening. Going quietly within is a time for integration that is very helpful in our relationships, but there's a lot of resistance to taking this time. One source of this resistance is our reluctance to change patterns of thinking and acting that we have developed over many years and that have served us pretty well. In chapter nine I discuss these patterns in more depth. Right now, I want to address our enormous reluctance to simply going within ourselves.

It is amazing that we spend 99% of our waking lives with our eyes open. When we go to sleep, we close our eyes; but when we're awake, we nearly always have them open. And so we miss the experience of being awake with our eyes closed. When we are awake with our eyes closed, we look inside instead of out. Our attention is drawn out primarily through our eyes, and if we close our eyes, we begin to go within. But we're actually programmed to fall asleep when we do that. When we're little we're told "Now it's time to go to sleep, close your eyes." What about saying:

"Now it's time to close your eyes and stay alert!"

Why don't we do this more often, why is it so strange

in our culture? The first reason is fear – a fear that derives from our evolution. Biologically we inhabit an animal body. We have human consciousness; but our heritage, our body, our physicality, is animal.

There have been very few generations, numerically, between us and the people who had no other culture than stone and bone. It's just a few thousand years ago, just a few hundred generations, which is not very long, biologically speaking. So on the physical, biological level, we are still Stone Age people.

Maybe we still live in fear of the sabre-toothed tiger!

Our bodies are programmed with a readiness for fear that is appropriate to living in the wilderness and in all the insecurity that goes along with that. The primary defence against the dangers of the wild is being able to see – so when we close our eyes we have to overcome a very natural fear.

Many people feel very afraid when you suggest to them "Close your eyes". They don't want to do it.

Try it outside, go to your local High Street and sit on a seat there, with your eyes closed. See if you feel comfortable or not. You'll feel afraid, some of the time at least.

Then there's a deeper level of fear, which is more to do with thinking, with the mind. When I am unaccustomed to being alert with my eyes closed, I don't know who I am when they are closed. I close my eyes and the external disappears, then I'm not the person that I am 99% of the time. There is a loss of identity.

When we close our eyes, we all experience the same thing – darkness. That's what we've done, we've shut out the light. We may see some patterns or after-images on the insides of our eyelids, colours or whatever, but essentially what happens when we close our eyes is that we experience darkness. It's the same for everybody; we go inside into darkness. And the darkness is full of a lot of fear for most of us, on very deep levels.

We experience who we are through our senses, and the sense that reaches out most is the sense of sight. When we take away the major sense, the sense of sight, there is fear. This fear needs to be confronted if we want to know about ourselves, if we want to explore our inner worlds.

I believe there is also an even deeper fear of going within, and that is the fear of infinity. Close your eyes and imagine going out with your sight, going out through the room, through the wall, across the town, across the sky, through the clouds, towards the sun or the moon or the stars. As you're going out there, you're going into the darkness, the same darkness that is inside you. Imagine going out into the stars, into the space between the stars, through the galaxy, going out of the galaxy, going through more darkness and more darkness, and you come to some more galaxies, and you go through them and beyond those, you're in more darkness and deeper darkness and wider, engulfing darkness. And it doesn't end, because you've passed through the furthest galaxy and you come to the other side of it, and there's still some nothingness there. Infinity stretches endlessly before you. I used to think about this when I was a little boy and terrify myself. I used to get very frightened. This infinite space is frightening to us, we prefer not to think about it. Come back to earth now, reverse the direction of your journey. Come back from beyond the distant galaxies, come back through the stars, through outer space to our solar system, to our planet, to your home. Come back now to the room you are in and to your body. That was quite a journey!

Now, if you want to continue, there's another, similar journey. Coming from outer space, enter into your own inner space. It's exactly the same thing. Close your eyes, and you can go into the darkness and go down inside, and it's equally infinite. On a simple physical level, you can go down into your body, into your organs. You can go down inside into the cellular level of your body where the cells are tiny, and you go into a cell and what the cell is comprised of is tiny, and you go into what that's comprised of and it's even tinier. Then into the molecules, then the atoms, and you go into what that is comprised of, the quarks and all these funny names that the physicists give to them, and that's even tinier, but what's half a quark? And what's half of a half of a quark? It doesn't end, does it? It can never end, can it? So even on the physical level, the infinity that we see or don't see, out there in the darkness, is the same if you go inward.

We're faced in two directions, inward and outward, by amazing nothingness, infinity, emptiness, darkness.

When we begin to go within we often have to face fear because this is so mysterious. We live our lives in such ordinary ways, we go to work and we look after the kids and we do the washing up and the cooking, earning the money, and we don't meet mystery very often. If you begin to think about this you may meet fear in different ways.

On one occasion when I was experimenting in meditation, I was in a hotel in India sharing a room with a friend and he went out, so I decided I would sit silently on the bed until he came back. I didn't know when that would be. He hadn't gone far, he hadn't left town, but it was maybe going to be an hour or two, so I decided I would sit quietly on the bed until he returned, as an experiment. I closed my eyes and sat still and quite soon the fear that I experienced was intense. I have never felt so afraid in my life; it was the deepest fear that I've ever felt.

Unwittingly, I had set up a battle within myself. A battle between my will and my fears. My mind produced a series of reasons why I should open my eyes: "Just open your eyes. There's no reason to keep you eyes closed any longer. You know its been long enough, hasn't it? And anyway he's gone off somewhere and he's not coming back." My mind was going crazy to try and get me to open my eyes. I didn't do it. Then it started on a physical level. "I've got a pain in my knee, I'd better move, I'd better stand up and shake my leg." I ignored that and that passed, and the next level was rational and reasonable, a voice in my head saying "Oh, it's time to stop now, it's fine, you've done enough and it has been at least an hour. How long have you got to do this?" I ignored that, and in the end I fantasised that there was a man in the room with a knife, and I was sweating with fear. I truly believed there was a man in the room with a knife. I heard the door open and somebody come in and I could hear him breathing, and I knew it wasn't the friend whom I was sharing the room with, because he was very noisy, and there was no way he could come into a room quietly. My whole body was pounding with fear, adrenalin coursing through me, and somehow I managed to ignore it, and sit with it. Of course it wasn't true, there wasn't a madman in the room with a knife about to kill me. It was an hallucination, a very powerful one, but just an hallucination. When I managed to ignore this, too, that was the final turn of the screw, the fear broke, and I passed into a place of bliss. Quietness. Unexpected. Unknown. A deep experience of timelessness and silence. I sat on with no further inner dispute, my mind and body both quiet and peaceful.

Where does this come from? It all happened inside me, all these things happened inside me and I didn't know anything about any of it beforehand. I just said "I'll sit down quietly for a while". There is a great mystery inside us, which we retreat from, because it's so enormous, it's so huge. Our little identity is so tiny compared to it, just like it is if you think of yourself compared to the size of the Earth.

We're a tiny speck of physicality and consciousness and yet we have contained in us this absolutely ineffable potential experience that all religions talk about.

Every branch of religion, every sect or cult that talks about inner experience all talk about the same thing.

They talk about something that happens inside us, to any one of us, and that can happen when we invite it. The basic way that you invite it is to go within, is to close your eyes; it's not surprising that we are afraid.

We don't have to understand it; but it's real. It's real in my experience. These peak experiences are open to us all. In my understanding, we are all of God, God is in all of us, we are all capable of experiencing the divine. It's inside, and it's experienced through going inside, going within.

There are hundreds of techniques for this. There are the one hundred and eight techniques of Shiva, an ancient set of Hindu techniques. The beads of the traditional Hindu *mala* are one hundred and eight beads, and they represent Shiva's one hundred and eight meditations. There are a plethora of these techniques available to us if we look. There are all sorts of things available to us but they're all basically different ways of going within and meeting this mystery, meeting this unknown inside us. We are alive in this body, having this opportunity, this potential, and we ignore it, try not to have it, work hard, in fact, not to have it.

When we stop doing that and turn to face what is inside us, so many troubles, so many difficulties just disappear, including many of the issues that create difficulties in our relationships.

If we're feeling so good today when we are experiencing the mystery that's inside us, the difficulties just dissolve, and we stop worrying about what's going to happen tomorrow. Just your heart beating, just that, you're inside, nothing else is happening, but you can feel your heart – bump, bump, bump. That's all you're feeling, you're not feeling anything else, nothing else is distracting you, it's like a miracle, an absolutely miraculous experience, simply being in the present moment.

I remember one time being in this place, and it was like being in a cathedral! I suppose I was somewhere in my ribcage, I don't know, but it was like this huge chamber, with this tremendous sound. Amazing! And that's just inside me, all I have to do is close my eyes. Well, I had to practise it for some days, but it's there, it's available to us. You're not worried about anything when you're internalised in this way, you're not worried about dying (that's the deep one), you're not worried about who you are, you're not worried about the difficulties and problems of your everyday life. If you take the opportunity to go within, you get your daily trials and tribulations in their proper perspective, which is small. Everything, everything is small, relative to what we can experience by going inside ourselves. We don't worry about those little slights that make us angry when we go deep inside. It's just not important.

And we appreciate life, we appreciate the beauty of life from in *here*.

Life is not out there, not in another beautiful person or a tree or a sunset, though these can be beautiful and appreciated, and centering in this way certainly makes you more open to connecting more deeply. Life is here, right inside you. Close your eyes, don't look at anything, listen to anything, just go inwards, and inwards, and inwards, and inwards; this is one of the deeper meanings of the symbolism of the cross.

Instead of being up here, in our heads, on this mental, thinking and emotional level, where we go to and fro, to and fro, you go down, down, down, down. In that moment, you're not in time any more. That's what the cross signifies. Along the horizontal is time-based exis-tence that goes on from moment to moment with all its difficulties, all its joys. Down the vertical, you go down inside, within; you go down in the moment and time is stopped. You're not concerned with time any more. It doesn't take long, not to be concerned with time. This is what the techniques of meditation are designed to help us do.

One of the things that I have really appreciated was that I was introduced to meditations that were physical-ly active. My notion of meditation before that was sitting still with my eyes closed and I thought people do that because they're afraid of life. Now I think the opposite. But I was introduced to meditation techniques that were physically active, where I could use my body and use my physical energy, and that was wonderful, really very helpful, because, for many people, to just sit still is extremely difficult and you can easily meet the kind of paranoid experience that I described happening to me. Many things are bubbling around in our bodies and in our emotions that can come up when we sit silently, and it can be very difficult just to sit and stay with it. Techniques of active meditation were consequently very helpful for me and I've seen them help thousands of other people as well.

One of these meditations involves shaking for fifteen minutes. You just allow your body to shake. There's nice music that goes with it, that encourages you to shake the body, and you just let the body shake for fifteen minutes, which is quite a long time. After about two minutes you think "Aren't we finished yet? This is going on a bit, I've been shaking long enough", and only three minutes have gone by! You think about something else, you space out for a bit and your body's shaking, and you come back and the music is still going on! Then the music changes and you begin fifteen minutes of dance or movement, allowing movement to happen through the body. The music comes in through the ears and the movement comes out through the feet or the arms or the head or whatever you feel like moving. Fifteen minutes doing that can feel quite long too, sometimes. The third fifteen minutes is sitting. Again with music, very peaceful, love-ly music. The fourth fifteen minutes is lying down, silent, with nothing, no accompaniment.

When I first used to do that meditation, mostly I'd fall asleep in the last stage. I think that's one of the reasons why it's good to meditate in the morning, because hope-fully, you've had a decent night's sleep, and it's easier to stay alert. But this kind of active technique was very helpful for me before being still. I recommend it in any form that you can find that appeals to you. You could try shaking, if you're going to sit. To allow some shaking or movement of the body beforehand can help you relax into it.

Sometimes we have to face a lot of demons when we go inside. We have to face aspects of our personal, individual unconscious and sometimes our collective unconscious as well. It may not be very comfortable, but it is a challenge. Am I going to do this or not? Or am I going to jump up from my fear that comes up inside and say "No, I'm not going to do that. No. No. I'll do that later"? In our relationships we often meet the demons named Fear of Commitment or Fear of Intimacy. Becoming more aware of them, and then choosing to meet and understand them more, can enhance our relationships in ways that are hard to imagine. So we have to meet these demons and we have to become more aware.

Awareness is a process of becoming more sensitive to oneself and one's body, this body of senses. As we go into it and experience it deeper and deeper, our senses are heightened, we become more sensitive, more sensual, and things affect us more deeply.

That too can be a challenge, because perhaps you've just been meditating and you feel very good, you've got a nice smile on your face and you feel very spiritual, very in touch with the deepest part of yourself. Then somebody treads on your toe, and BOOM! a sudden rush of anger comes up. Whoops, there goes my image of myself as this spiritual, loving being! Your defences, your old conditionings, are being pulled apart by going within. Suddenly you're challenged with that.

This process of going within makes you more sensitive.

It makes you more sensitive to love, it makes you more sensitive to beauty, and everything that you're experiencing is heightened. This is both beautiful and very challenging and so it can be very difficult to allow. It's as though we're a sort of narrow band receiver, and we keep it narrow because we can stay in control and know who and where we are, that we're in this narrow band of reception. If you follow this path of going within, it starts to widen out. You don't have control over it in the same way as you had previously, and you have to let go of what and who you think you are, because, *whatever it is you think you are, you are not that.*

That's not who you are. Whatever it is you think you are is a limitation, it's less than what you are.

For example, when we go within, each one of us, if we just close our eyes and go into that dark, we go to the same place. I go to the same place that you go to in there. You go through your identity, your individuality, and so do I. But when I go through that, when I pass deep beyond that, we're all in the same place, we're all in that infinite place, that dark, which is where everything comes from. Everything arises out of this black, dark, empty place inside each one of us. And that is the ground, the source; and it's the same in you, it's the same in me. It isn't any different. It has the same qualities, it has the qualities of truth and love and beauty. They're all the same in each of us, or through each of us. It's not different. We all have that same root in both spellings of the word: the route as a path, and the root as the root of a tree or a plant going down into the earth, into the darkness. We all have that, we have the same possibility; the same avenue is available to us. There is only one way to know this for yourself and that is to do it. In doing it we connect to the deeper truth of being alive and this helps us to be less anxious and demanding in our relationships. I encourage you to try the exercise that follows.

▶ **EXERCISE 5**

An introduction to meditation

This is a simple technique to introduce you to meditation and to going within. You can do it for a couple of minutes or longer, up to half an hour. I suggest ten minutes to start with. First, make sure you won't be disturbed for the allotted time – switch off the telephone. Second, make sure that you are sitting or lying comfortably. There's no need to be uncomfortable, it helps to be at ease physically. I suggest you get a timing device and set it for ten minutes. If you have no timing device you could put on some music that lasts for a set time, say a track of five minutes, and let that be your timer. The important thing is to put the timing outside of yourself so that you can focus inwards without distraction. If you use music make it soft instrumental music that will be in the background. You don't want to give it your attention. Your attention is going to be on your breathing.

What you are going to do is count your breath. Let the breath be easy and natural. You count one for the first in-breath, two for the out-breath, three for the next in-breath, and so on up to nine, then the next out-breath is zero, and the following in-breath begins at one again. You can repeat this cycle counting the breaths up to nine and then re-starting at zero for the next ten minutes. This is all you do, nothing else. There has been some research that showed that counting in single digits only occupies a small part of the brain – allowing you to count and relax at the same time.

It's best to do it with eyes closed, as it's easier to focus on the breath. However, it's not necessary. If you wish to have your eyes open, that's OK. Look down a few feet in front of you and let your eyes be unfocused. Put your attention on counting your breath.

This is a good introduction to meditation. However, its very simplicity often leads to difficulties. Many of us want to complicate it. Though it is simple, it's not necessarily easy. Only counting the breath is a very minimal level of activity for us. We are accustomed to doing much more. Please don't add anything to the technique, let it stand as it is.

A problem that is often reported is that "I lose track of the numbers, I drift off and start thinking about something else." Don't worry if that happens, stick to the technique. As soon as you notice that you've gone off, in that moment of noticing, you're back. Simply start counting again. As you do it more often, you will find it easier to stay with the breath.

At the end of the allotted time, come back and take a moment to see how you are feeling, how your body is, and how your mind is. Stand up and shake your body a little, stamp your feet a few times, look around and know that you are present in this moment.

(There is an audiotape 'An Introduction to Meditation' available. Details are at the back of the book.)

When we start to be aware of our ability to deceive, then we are also starting to be aware of our ability to know truth.

ARE WE NATURAL BORN LIARS?

When we go inside, we begin to know truth from there. With some awareness of our emotions, particularly our fear, anger and pain, and a willingness to know the mystery that is inside us, we are going a long way towards being more honest, more true to ourselves. We can then bring this quality to our relationships. It is in the garden of truth that intimacy grows. In being honest with ourselves we start to respect truth and only then can we learn to recognise the truth in others. As already mentioned, the wonderful words "I love you" can be said deceitfully. We need to be able to hear whether what is being said to us in intimacy is the truth or deceit because in intimacy we are at our most vulnerable and therefore most potentially gullible.

The first step in differentiating between truth and deceit is to see why the ability to deceive is such an important part of all of us. Great amounts of our energy, internally and externally, as a society, are taken up with this fact – that we are great deceivers.

Human beings are very good at deceit. We're so good at deception that we deceive ourselves a lot of the time.

We don't have much consciousness about our ability to lie. I don't hear people talking about it except in a very condemnatory way, usually about other people, not ourselves. Be honest with yourself right now. How truthful are you? I don't hear people relating to this, yet it is a very important fact about us all.

One of the bases of being human is the ability to be deceptive, the ability to deceive others.

In my reading about the development of humanity, there's a big question mark in biology and paleoanthropology over why we developed a big brain as we evolved from the other primates. There's a sudden huge increase in the size of the brain, from about five or six hundred grams to double that, and this happened quite suddenly as far as the scientists can tell. It seems to me that one of the reasons this might be is that with the development of language comes the ability to lie, and therefore an increasingly complex need for humans to understand that other people might be lying. I imagine a scene in which a prehistoric hunter brings a message in the earliest form of communication, perhaps a drawing in the dust, or some simple sound that tells his tribe that there is a hunting opportunity on the other side of the hill, out of sight. The people he or she is telling may walk into a trap if it is a lie. If they aren't aware of the possibility of deception then they are vulnerable to an ambush and therefore are less likely to be successful in a competitive environment where the fittest survive. The fittest, in this case, will be those who can recognise the possibility of deceit and guard against it. This requires a highly developed imagination and ability to conceptualise which would encourage the growth of these faculties in our brains.

In Jane Goodall's book *In the Shadow of Man*, about her studies of chimpanzees, she describes a baby chimpanzee seeing an adult chimpanzee digging up a root. The baby then makes a noise as though it's being attacked, and its mother, who's nearby but not within sight, appears on stage, as it were, takes in the scene, and assumes that the other adult chimpanzee has attacked her baby. She therefore jumps on the other adult, who runs away, and the baby trots over and gets the root!

I've always remembered this little cameo in particular, because it seemed to me to demonstrate an incredible complexity in the brain of this little chimp which we tend to think is not very intelligent compared to us. This little baby chimpanzee is, first of all, able to see the possibility of deception. In some way, it sees that "If I do this, then I might be able to get that, because this might happen." This is quite a complex chain of thought. And not only is he able to think that through or to see the possibility of it, but he's also able to execute it. It doesn't work if the chimpanzee doesn't do it properly. If he fails to deceive, his mother might come and bash him instead – so the chimpanzee has not only got to conceive it and see the possibility, he's got to execute it. He's got to deceive effectively, in order to get what he wants.

If we take that ability into human society, we've got to have very complex faculties of imagination to think about what the other person might be going to do, in order to protect ourselves. We have to think about the truth of the other person in terms of their behaviour, in terms of their actions, in terms of what they're saying. This seems to me to be one of the possible reasons which would explain this tremendous spurt of growth in the brain.

This ability to deceive has its place – it's not something to condemn or deny – and it comes from our animal heritage along with the fact that we're born into a body. Many animals are great deceivers and base their survival on this. The fox is renowned for its cunning, for example. And how about the moth that doesn't look like a moth any more when its wings are open? It has what looks like two large eyes that make it appear huge in the dark, so that any creature that might want to eat it will mistake it for something too big to attack. That's the theory, and it does work, of course. Those creatures that have the ability to deceive do survive. Humans have these abilities, too.

I believe it is the capacity for *consciousness* about the difference between truth and deceit that differentiates us from animals.

When we start to be aware of our ability to deceive, then we are also starting to be aware of our ability to know truth.

That is when we start to leave behind the animal part of our heritage, and take a path towards God. Humans are somewhere between animals and God, and truth is one of the paths that takes us in the direction of the divine.

In human culture, if we look at the example of the judicial system, it is actually based on our ability to deceive. If we didn't have this deceptive ability, we wouldn't need the system. We would simply ask for the truth and it would be told. We wouldn't need juries or lawyers. Perhaps we'd still need somebody to be a referee or an arbiter to make a fair decision in cases of dispute, but that is a very minor part of a judicial system. The vast part of the system is only there because of our ability to deceive. The court tries to make some decisions about whether someone is telling the truth, in order that it can make a judgment. But the purpose of the court – its primary purpose – is actually to make a judgment; its main purpose is not truth. If you've ever been to a court, or seen it on the television, you'll know that the processes that take place in court are often lies, and they're lies for the purpose of winning. The primary purpose of lawyers is to get a favourable judgment, not necessarily to find out the truth. They will produce all kinds of arguments that they know are not true in order to influence the situation. This is not a respect for truth as I understand it. It's a desire for judgment, which is to do with the mind.

If we want truth, we must come out of the mind to connect to truth, which is not in the mind. The mind thinks about this or that, right or wrong, yes or no, good or bad – that's one of the functions of the mind, to move between polarities. Truth is somewhere deeper inside; it's not about having a logical argument where you end up being convinced, it's a deeper experience of truth which is more than just thinking. The body, which is our animal heritage, is also the place in which we can *feel* whether something's true or not, whether it has the ring of truth, whether it sounds true. The mind is not very helpful in that regard, it's too easily deceived.

We have a deeper place inside us – the heart – which has a different sense of whether something's true. And in order to connect with that, one of the things we have to do is to stop listening so much to the mind. We have to come to some deeper place inside us, which can feel or sense "Is this true or not?" "Do I have a sense of truth when I hear this?" We have an innate faculty that has a relationship to truth. We can sense truth in the same way that we sense beauty. This is not an analytical faculty, it's not something that allows us to analyse the situation logically and come to a conclusion that says "This is true or untrue". It is a different faculty which is more intuitive, which says "This has the ring of truth." Something has the ring of truth, or a sense of rightness, just as we might have a feeling of beauty about something. When we follow this feeling or intuitive faculty, we go inside ourselves in a new or deeper way, which is very important on this path of growth. We develop our consciousness of God or the divine, our ability to know the divine, to experience the divine here, in the body. This consciousness of me, of I, of this self, whatever words you want to use for it, is related to conscience, to having an awareness of how our actions affect others, or affect the world out there, and of when we have done something wrong. As we develop our consciousness we also develop our conscience; if we tell a lie, for example, then we will feel something inside, some kind of shame or remorse.

People who don't feel that, who are without those feelings inside, are often described as psychopathic, and they do end up, many of them, behaving in what we might label a psychopathic fashion. They don't have any ability to feel remorse, and therefore they do terrible things. They really are very ill, because they lack this ability to feel what we call conscience.

So, here we are now, we're in this body which is an animal body, and one of the ways in which we transcend the animal body or move forward from it is by being conscious of the truth. This takes us toward the divine, the divinity that exists in us, that is available to us because we've got this body. This is the paradox: because of the animal heritage we have both the ability to deceive, and also the ability to see or to feel, to perceive or experience the truth. We have both these abilities. But the second one needs consciousness and it needs conscious intention, to develop it.

The way to do this is through the body, which is our root, our root into the ground, our foundation into truth. Through it, we somehow experience these things about truth and consciousness. It's a great place to root ourselves. I think we have been, in many ways, actually driven from our bodies, because many of us had a lot of painful experiences as we were growing up and these have tended to make us want to withdraw in some way from our bodies.

We withdrew from our parents when we had painful experiences, we withdrew from our relationship with them. It's as though we started to live a few feet away, behind our own bodies, because it was a bit safer, because we didn't want to feel the pain. We believed we needed to defend ourselves from the pain, so it's an appropriate thing to do, to pull out, to back off, to be out of the body. But when we get to a point in our lives where we want to start to have a better relationship with truth, we start to need to come back into the body in order to sense with the body. That often brings us in touch with a lot of feelings from the past that are painful or difficult in some way; but that, I think, is necessary, and has to be passed through. It helps us to be more compassionate with ourselves and others when we know about the pain of being alive, when we know our vulnerability and the ease with which we can hurt and be hurt. That intimate knowledge of pain from our own experience provides us with the base from which we can identify with other people, understand their difficulties, and be less rejecting and less judgemental, more accepting and more forgiving.

You can demonstrate this ability to separate from your body right now. You can imagine standing outside yourself and seeing yourself. For example, I can experience myself right now as sitting here in this chair. Here I am, I'm sitting here in this chair and if I speak my mouth is opening, my tongue is moving and my throat is doing these wonderful things that it does to produce sound, and my hands are moving, and I can know I am doing all these things even if I close my eyes; I know it from the inside. We can all do this, at any time that we choose to do this, we can somehow stand aside from ourselves and know. You can say "I'm going inside my body". This is consciousness.

This ability to be conscious is the essence of being human.

I know that I'm sitting here and there's a little bit of tension in my buttocks as I sit here. I can experience this. Or I can feel something in my shoulder, or my elbows, or my knees. This is being able to be conscious of what's going on in the body. You can do it, too. As you are reading you can be aware of tension, in your arm perhaps, or in your forehead or leg, or wherever.

When we start to do these things, we start to have a new awareness, a deeper awareness. We can deepen this with our intention, by choosing to go within, to go into the body. And the body, even though it has this animal heritage of deception, is the place of truth. Truth is in the body somewhere, somehow – you might need to decode it – but the body is the place where you will find the truth. The truth will come out through allowing yourself to experience what is in your body.

The musculature of the body even contains memories of experience that you had in the past that you have completely forgotten. There's been a lot of research on this, a whole sphere of psychotherapy called *bioenergetics,* which is based on the fact that we have a form of musculature which has to do with our experience and how we've developed, which gives us a particular shape. (See *Bioenergetics* by Alexander Lowen or *Bodymind* by Ken Dychwald.)

If we give the body loving attention it will reward us with the truth. The importance of this that I want to emphasise is that we need to have this ability to see, to sense, to know the truth in order to get our relationships right.

If we don't have it, we won't get them right. People can tell us lies, and we'll believe them, and we'll be deceived. At the beginning of the chapter I posed the question "Are we natural born liars?" My answer to this is that we are all born with the capacity to lie, therefore it's up to us as individuals whether we lie or not. In a recent workshop when we were discussing this, there were objections to the idea that small children were natural liars. We heard a lovely anecdote from one mother whose six-year-old daughter had come home from school in a complete daze because she discovered the truth about lying! A little boy had hit her and when challenged by the teacher he had flatly denied it. The little girl had never seen the possibility of lying before that and was utterly surprised. The mother ended the story by saying that she'd had a lot of difficulty for a while as her daughter experimented with this new concept and started lying herself. This beautiful innocence is something we all have to lose.

We need to have the ability to recognise deception. If we're in a relationship with somebody who doesn't have a respect for truth, then that's very, very difficult. If that's the case, you need to know that in order to protect yourself. If you don't know that, then you can't even begin to make it better, to change it for yourself.

Nothing destroys intimacy quicker than lies. And nothing nourishes it better than truth. In order to protect ourselves from being deceived we have to negotiate this ability all the time, both in ourselves and in our relationships. We have to ask ourselves both "Am I being truthful?" and "Is this other person being truthful?"

We have to be conscious of whether or not we actually believe the other. If we go in the naive direction, where we tend to believe everybody, we're in just as much trouble as if we went in the other direction, the suspicious end of the spectrum, where no-one is believed.

Both positions have their own difficulties, and a place needs to be found somewhere in the middle, where there is more balance, where not everything is necessarily believed nor everything necessarily suspected. For example, if, because somebody says "I love you", you take that to be true, you'll often find yourself in trouble. Many women have been taken in by men saying this to them in order to cheat them into having sex with them. It's sad to say, but I think it has been, and still may be, a fairly common experience. Equally, if somebody says "I love you", and you're immediately suspicious, this isn't going to get you very far in an intimate relationship. We have to operate on this continuum and it is especially important in intimate relationships.

We have, and can develop within us, the ability to

know the truth. We need to develop for ourselves our own capacity to know 'the ring of truth', for our own understanding of ourselves and the world – our inner world as well as our outer world – and also for our relationships. Then we can begin to trust from a more secure foundation. If you think about the earlier chapter on listening, there's no point in communicating well with somebody if you don't believe them. If what's being said in your opinion is rubbish, then communication is not going to go very far.

As we listen when a person is speaking to us, we decide whether what we are hearing is truthful in a way that is not logical; it's not a logical analysis, it's more a sense of truth. Equally, we need to be aware of the opposite: whether what that person is saying is false. We have to develop that sense.

When we engage in this we are in a process of learning about the truth. We start off by realising "I don't want to pretend any more, this pretence isn't getting me anywhere", and saying to ourselves:

"My intention is to be as honest as I can. I want to have truth as a value, as a passion, and I measure my truthfulness in the fire of relationships."

This isn't about being brutally honest with people. It *is* about some kind of heartfelt, compassionate truth, not only with the other but with oneself. We have to deal with what's within ourselves, and if we have a passionate and compassionate attitude toward ourselves in relation to truth, that will start to be reflected in our relationships. And then our relationships start to have the kind of nourishing, supportive quality that we deserve.

> **▶ EXERCISE 6**

A truth exercise

A   Take some private time to yourself with some paper and
a pen. Remember a time when you lied – write a brief
account of it. Now notice what your feelings are. Is
shame part of this experience? Regret? Defiance? Fear?
Write a little about your feelings now and also about
your feelings at the time. Ask yourself why you lied.
Why was it necessary? Know that it WAS necessary to
some important part of you, regardless of how you
might judge yourself. What purpose did lying serve?

B   Now remember a time when someone lied to you.
Follow the same process as above. Make sure you write
about your feelings, not about what you imagine the
other person was feeling. Focus on your feelings about
being lied to. Are you angry? Hurt? Confused? Afraid?
Were you naive? Were you too innocent, too trusting?

C   Read through both accounts and your responses and
see if you can expand your consciousness about them.
See if you can move away from judgement towards a
more heartful and compassionate view. It may help,
even if they are recent, to view these events as though
they were a long, long time ago and to know or
imagine that you have moved on in your development
and to see them shrinking into whatever their proper
place is in your life, a place where you are learning from
your mistakes, and are able to be more forgiving. Let go

of the judgements you have, both about yourself and the person or people involved. Don't worry if you can't; put the writing away and come back to it later, after a week or two. See what happens then.

Whatever you do, or dream you can do, begin it. All this has genius, power, and magic in it. Begin it now. GOETHE

AGREEMENTS FROM THE WORLD

As we follow this path into ourselves, looking at our feelings, respecting truth, being curious about ourselves as humans, something mysterious starts to happen more and more, something called synchronicity. This is when events coincide, but are more than coincidence, where something is happening that is inexplicable to the logical mind. We have all had this experience. It often has a physical component like feeling a prickling sensation in the upper spine and neck. Some people dismiss it as 'coincidence' but that is probably because they are unhappy about not being able to explain it. Synchronicity is an example of a larger phenomenon that I call 'agreements from the world'. They are an essential part of the human experience. They are very important because they're so mysterious and so inexplicable; and yet we have all experienced them in some form or another. They have the flavour of the beyond, or the divine.

I think that's just what they are – an intrusion into the very neatly ordered world that we're desperately trying to keep under control. They are an intrusion into that order by something much bigger, a much larger order. They are a little nudge from what I call the 'cosmic elbow' saying "I'm going to knock down your pile of dominoes if you keep standing them up in that way."

Agreements from the world are very important. A couple of things happened as I was writing this book that I would like to share with you as examples. When I was writing the chapter about going within I asked myself "What's half a quark? It has to be something, if it's there, if it exists, if it has a material existence then there has to be something that exists that's half of it. The only problem is whether it can be seen, sensed or measured." And that partly motivated the idea of the visualisation of going into the infinity of one's own physical body.

Later that week there was an article by Danny Penman and Charles Arthur on the front page of *The Independent*, which said:

"Scientists think that the basic constituent of matter, long thought to be called quarks, is made of something smaller. Quarks, whose mass is less than a million, million, billionth times less than a grain of sand, are not the tiniest things the universe has to offer."

The journalists were writing about the fact that, logically, quarks must have some kind of internal structure. Scientists are now looking for a more fundamental particle than the 'most' fundamental. I thought that was a lovely example of an agreement from the world: to see, on the front page of *The Independent*, a report about 'half a quark' at the same time that I'd been thinking about it. I had a feeling of being in touch with some kind of current of thought or feeling or knowledge that was bigger than just me, the individual. It felt good.

Then, when writing about truth and deceit, which I consider to be completely crucial to intimate relationships and to the path of growth and personal under-standing, I opened the newspaper to find a transcript of one of the Reith Lectures by Jean Aicheson on the BBC, called "Why Deception is the Mother of Speech" (*The Independent,* February 14th 1996). She wrote:

"We use language to convey information, but one of its main uses is to enable us to lie."

In her article she said that language is good for certain things but, in particular:

"It's especially good for interacting with others and influencing them, and an effective persuader must be able to imagine events from another person's point of view."

She went on to say that humans differ from animals in their ability to deceive; mainly, as she puts it, because:

"Humans can use deception for good purposes, for reasons of tact or diplomacy."

They can also, she said: "...calculate how to influence others and how to please them", and that this ability is actually crucial in the formation of language. She partic-ularly pointed to the fact that language gives us the abil-ity to talk convincingly about things which are absent or even nonexistent. It is an obvious survival benefit to be able quickly to communicate to other people that there is a sabre-toothed tiger just over the hill out of sight. At the same time it is possible to imagine that the same communication could be a lie designed to make the lis-teners run away for some reason that would benefit the speaker.

For me, this was another agreement from the world, where I felt that what I was doing was being supported in a mysterious way, as well as being validated by a respected academic. Where it leads to for me is a sense that if I live my life in some *proper* way, then I will receive agreements from the world that will help me to do that and will help me to find direction. They will be supportive of what I'm doing.

So, what do I mean by 'in a *proper* way'? Living a proper life is, to me, a very compassionate concept; compassionate to me, compassionate to you, and to the people around me with whom I'm in contact. This style of life where I am endeavouring to come closer and closer to the truth within me has a wonderful flow with which we can connect, and we can't do it just through our minds. Our minds have some part to play in it; I couldn't be sitting here writing this if I wasn't using my mind; you wouldn't be reading and making sense of it, without using your mind. But the mind as a controller or as a censor can interfere with us joining this flow. There's a wonderful quotation from Goethe which is about joining in the flow of life and the mysterious rewards that come to us when we do:

"Until one is motivated, there is hesitancy. The chance to draw back, always ineffectiveness. Concerning all acts of initiative and creation, there is one elementary truth, the ignorance of which kills countless ideas and splendid plans. The moment one definitely commits oneself, then Providence moves too. All sorts of things occur to help one that would never otherwise have occurred, a whole stream of events issue from the decision, raising in one's favour all manner of unforeseen incidents and meetings and material assistance which no man could have dreamed would come. Whatever you do, or dream you can do, begin it. All this has genius, power, and magic in it. Begin it now."

This is a very inspiring piece of writing; what it means

to me is that unless we start to take hold of our lives in that kind of way, we can't join this flow. Unless we are willing to commit ourselves, say, to an existing relationship, a change in ourselves, a project with another, or to understanding a child's problems from their point of view, then we limit ourselves.

I believe that life itself urges us to live *properly*. This may include agreements from the world that are not always pleasant, that sometimes feel harsh – they don't necessarily feel like *agreements* at all, because sometimes we are resisting and not listening to what life is telling us. The world will often disagree with our thinking because our minds are rather small and the world is rather large, and we need to be made aware of our limitations. The more we grasp and cling on to our limitations, then the more agreements from the world will feel horrible to us, will feel like disagreements.

Earlier on in my life, I felt knocked around by events and I used to imagine a 'cosmic elbow' which would suddenly appear out of a cloud and whack me around the ear, and throw me in the ditch; it was not a very pleasant experience! My first major experience of it was when my first marriage ended. It was very painful. I felt that my life was out of control, and that I was being pushed around by circumstances much bigger than me. I couldn't see at the time that anything good would come from it, but it did. I felt compelled to go deep into therapy and meditation and it was a huge impetus towards healing.

That was, in my present way of looking at it, an agreement from the world. I needed to go through those experiences because I was getting in my own way, or getting in the way of the flow. I was too identified with being a father and a husband, I wasn't my own man, I knew very little of myself, I was too busy trying to live up to other people's expectations of me.

It makes sense to try to get in line with the flow of life, which is a lot bigger than we are, because it feels better, it's enjoyable and it's more pleasant than continuously getting knocked down. The 'cosmic elbow' basically whacks us on the head and says "Wake up! Wake up! You're not the centre of the universe!" I *am* the centre of my life, but I'm *not* the centre of the universe. We have to let go of the idea that we are the most important thing around. We have to learn a kind of surrender, and at the same time acknowledge that this letting go rests with each one of us, and that no-one can do this for us. We have to surrender. We have to give in – but we mustn't give up.

We have to find ways to let go, with awareness, knowing that this is our life, that nobody else can or will do it for us. Nobody can run our lives for us. That doesn't mean to say that other people can't help us find out more about ourselves and life; other people of course can help. But we have to take our lives in our own hands, and at the same time offer them up. Give them up to the flow, or to God or to the divine. This is a complete paradox: we have to do both things. We have to take our life as our own and also give in to the flow and power of life that is so much greater than we are.

I think the only way we have peace is when we take on this challenge. If we don't take it on, then we suffer. This is the result of not taking it on, because the flow of life, as I understand it, is saying "Take it on". If we refuse, we become stuck with suffering. If we take it on, we will probably have to pass through some suffering in order to heal things within us that need to be healed. To me there is an appropriateness about that kind of suffering, it's a suffering that has some quality of rightness. It creates some sense that things are moving in a good direction, even though it may feel horrible. Whereas the other route, where I refuse to accept the push, or the flow, of life, brings with it stuckness, a sense of wrongness. An example of this would be ending a relationship, which is sometimes very hard to do, even when we know in our heart that it is the best thing. Actually doing this can be extremely painful perhaps because there has been love between you in the past and so we delay and resist and suffer more than we need to as a result.

It's not necessarily action 'out there' that I'm talking about. It might be, but it isn't necessarily. There's a great pressure on us in our culture towards action, towards doing. What's the great merit in that? There's sometimes great merit in not doing things, in non-doing or in nothingness. So much of the suffering and difficulty in the world and in our lives come from things that are being *done*. If we sat down more, gave ourselves some time for reflection and relaxation, for not doing anything, things might be a bit more balanced.

If there is no obvious action that your inner sense of truth leads you to, then take the option of doing nothing. Try that option, it's a powerful one. But we are really hung up on action; we're hung up on decisiveness, on the idea that we *should* know what to do.

"I don't know!" It's a wonderful place to be; but it's totally ignored and discounted in our culture.

We are afraid of not knowing. Something inside us says "I don't like being in this place, I'm going to decide something, I'm going to get out of this place in me."

That's fear speaking. There's a big fear in us of doing nothing, of not knowing. And what *do* we know, when it comes down to it?

I am not invalidating the position of action, I am just supporting the position of inaction because it gets a bad press. So give it a try. In the end, you are the centre of your life, and only you know what's best for you. That's not to say that somebody can't help you by some inter-action, that some things may not be made clearer to you. But still it comes down to you – that other person or those other people aren't going to take care of it for you.

Socrates said "We need to free ourselves from thinking that we know, when we don't." When we do this, we open ourselves to the mysterious support of the universe. We open ourselves to agreements from the world. We may find the 'cosmic elbow' a bit harsh at times, but, in my experience, it's for the best. When we consciously choose to align ourselves with the flow of life, this is a fundamental change of perception. We are not in con-trol, however much we would like to imagine that we are. This is not to say that we are helpless; when we apply our consciousness, we have great freedom and opportunity. We can choose to invite the mysterious into our lives to support us and our relationships. It's a form of trust in life, a belief and an affirmation that life is essentially positive. When we trust, we make ourselves available to miracles.

▸ EXERCISE 7

Synchronicity remembered

This exercise will be more effective if done with a partner. Bring back to mind times when you have experienced 'agreements from the world'. Write brief accounts of them that are not critical or judgemental in any way. Note what happened in your body as you recall (and if with a partner, share) these events. The most common effects are shivers up the spine, bristling of hairs on neck and/or arms and other parts of the body. Pay attention also to other parts of the body, the solar plexus, the lower stomach –'the guts', the eyes, and the knees. Also, notice your breathing and any muscle tensions. All these effects are body responses acknowledging the power of the unknown, of the beyond. Some of them are primitive responses, others more sophisticated. Become more familiar with these effects and the events that cause them; become more friendly with these moments of adventure when the unexplained becomes the experienced. Invite this more into your life and your relationships in these ways and you invite a deeper quality of experience into your life.

We can choose to change any thought that we feel is not supporting us in our journey, right now.

AFFIRMATIONS AS INVOCATIONS

The statement at the beginning of this book – *I deserve a loving and supportive relationship* – is a positive affirmation. This whole book is an affirmation of my belief that all people deserve this. It is an idea that most people can agree with when it is phrased generally as "We all deserve loving and supportive relationships." Unfortunately, many of us are not experiencing this; far from it. Most people have an aspect of blame and sef-doubt that says "If I'm not being loved it must be my fault somehow." Or, "If I'm not being loved, it's someone else's fault and there's nothing I can do about it." So the very personal – *I deserve a loving and supportive relationship* – is a statement that is likely to provoke disagreement. Positive affirmations, used properly (and the use of them is widely misunderstood), can be a very deep route to understanding your situation better and the reality of how you may be contributing to what's happening. They are also a powerful way of invoking the mysterious support of life.

I first came across the use of affirmations about fifteen years ago, in connection with a breathing technique

called 'rebirthing'. A common phrase I was asked to use
was: "It's easier and easier for me to breathe more
freely." I thought it was some sort of self-hypnosis,
which wasn't in the least bit helpful. I couldn't see any
point in repeating, parrot-fashion, something that didn't
seem to be true. Unfortunately the people who were
teaching these techniques didn't explain how and why
they work. That was a great shame, because now, after
twenty years of experience of many different therapy
techniques, I see affirmations as very useful and very
powerful.

We're actually using affirmations all the time. Most of
what we think is an affirmation in one way or another. If
we are repeatedly thinking something inside ourselves –
the kinds of thoughts that we have on most days – we are
unconsciously affirming something about ourselves, our
lives, our relationships or our work. If we often think a
particular thought, or set of thoughts, then we are more
strongly confirming the beliefs that these thoughts represent. We may want to change these thoughts if they are
negative. I would like to encourage you to become more
conscious of what it is that you're thinking and affirming.
Having become more conscious, you can then take some
action to change it, if you wish.

I used to have a thought that ran through my mind for
many years, which was: "I don't believe it". When I
started to examine it, I discovered that this thought "I
don't believe it" gave me some control over my reality.
Something would happen in my life, and I could say to
myself "I don't believe it". It didn't matter if it was true
or not, because if I could say to myself "I don't believe
it", this gave me some sense of control. At that early age
this was useful to me but as I grew up it became less use ful

and more of an unconscious negative affirmation. If you listen out for this phrase, you will hear it often. People say it as a way of lessening the impact of events, both negative and positive: "Mr Lucky, you've just won first prize." "I don't believe it!" Or when someone dies you may have a strong sense of disbelief as a form of protection. There is another aspect, too, which represents a cynical attitude, a tendency to suspicion and mistrust. It is easy to scoff at things and say " I don't believe it".

When I examined this attitude more deeply, what I found was that it developed when I was very young, in my relationship with my sister. My big sister – she was four years older than me – used to tease me a lot, and the only power that I had over this situation was to use my imagination and say to myself "I don't believe this is happening". So this particular strategy went back deep into my past, and as an adult it manifested in me as cynicism, suspicion, mistrust, and in my use of the phrase "I don't believe it". When I understood this better I decided to change it. It was much better, more mature, to start to look into things and to see if they were true rather than automatically dismiss them as untrue, even if they were difficult or uncomfortable for me. Soon this phrase "I don't believe it" started to disappear from my mind. It is hardly ever there now; in fact almost never.

This was an example of a negative affirmation that had been in my life for a long time. I was able to change a pattern which went back more than thirty years through using my consciousness in the present.

Another example of the use of affimations is the placing of a sign on your wall with an inspiring message. I have an affirmation on the wall that says "I deserve the best". What this affirmation continually does for me is to

provoke thoughts and ideas about the statement "I
deserve the best". It's there on my mantelpiece and I see
it every day; I am reminded of it both consciously and
subconsciously. I don't need to be actually conscious of
seeing it for it to have an effect. We all appreciate beautiful things around us but we don't have to be conscious
of their presence for them to have an effect. It's the same
with written affirmations. Since it has been there, I think
more and more: "What does it mean? What does the
best mean to me? What does it mean in my thoughts, in
my actions, in my life?" I am stimulated into reflecting
on my values.

It is also an interesting affirmation because it uses the
words "I deserve" (as in "I deserve a loving and supportive relationship, or loving and supportive relationships"). As I said before, I believe this is a simple truth,
we *do* all deserve loving and supportive relationships. It's
true for all of us. And this is because we exist, because
we breathe, because we were born, and came into our
bodies; we don't have to do anything more to deserve life
and loving relationships.

The fact that we need to affirm this positively shows
that on some level we don't really believe it, and that in
some ways we're manifesting our disbelief. However,
that doesn't make it untrue, it simply means that we've
had negative, painful experiences of relationships in the
past, and have developed negative ideas and beliefs based
on those experiences. But these beliefs can be changed.
Even if we continue to be in painful relationships in our
present lives, we can still do something about it. It's very
helpful to use a powerful statement like "I deserve a loving and supportive relationship" to contradict our inner
disbelief, to help us to address an absence of love in our

lives, whatever relationship we're in.

If we have a pattern of thinking that we want to change we can do something about it now, in the present. We can do this because they're *our* thoughts and we can have the thoughts that we choose. We can interrupt our stream of consciousness and choose to think and affirm something different when we hear ourselves expressing sayings and beliefs we want to change.

This is very important.

We can choose to change any thought that we feel is not supporting us in our journey, right now.

Affirmations, as I use them in my workshops, can be very helpful in this process, because negative patterns of thinking and behaviour often go very far back into our past, and we need something strong to help us contradict them.

In fact, we *only* need to use positive affirmations about things we *don't* believe. They are a technique for addressing our negative beliefs. When we use affirmations what we're actually doing is creating a friction inside us. We have a habit of thought or a habit of behaviour that we may have had for a long time that is in contradiction to the new, positive affirmation. If you start to change that habit, what happens is that you have an inner conflict between the old and the new ideas. The friction exists because the new idea that you are affirming directly contradicts your old negative beliefs and your past experience.

Being up against the old beliefs, the positive affirmation will bring out memories, thoughts and all kinds of feelings. The purpose of affirmations is to bring out whatever past experience is informing our present-day negative statements, beliefs and behaviours. Many old experiences are buried in our unconscious and remain there, affecting and colouring our attitudes to life and to ourselves. As long as they are unconscious we can do little directly to change them. Any method that helps us bring these to light is a great boon.

However, this is not a comfortable process, it's a friction technique which creates discomfort inside us. It's an apparent contradiction, that when we're using this wonderful positive statement, it seems to be having a negative effect. But that's not what's actually happening; it's not a negative effect. What's emerging from us *may* be negative, but it *needs* to be brought out, it needs to be seen and brought into consciousness so that we can be free of it, so we can say "Thank you" to it for protecting us and then let it go because we no longer need it. If we don't fully understand this, there may be a temptation to give up because affirmations don't necessarily immediately make us feel good and positive, in fact, our lives may seem to be getting worse, not better. That's a great shame, because in fact this discomfort means the affirmations are really working!

It's important to be open to things coming up, or your affirmation going deeper in, which is the same thing. When things come up from inside us, the affirmation is going deeper. The first thing is that we need to be open to that, we need to affirm that this is OK, even if it's uncomfortable.

Another particular strength of positive affirmations as a technique is that they are very much under your control. You can use them as much or as little as you choose, and therefore change at a pace that you find appropriate.

The statements in the earlier chapter on emotions can be used as positive affirmations. "Anger has a place in my life" is a confronting statement that challenges us to examine our beliefs and behaviour to find a way to integrate anger. The same applies to fear and pain. If we repeat these statements to ourselves we can begin to understand these feelings and their role in our lives.

In my workshops I consider this to be crucial, and I create situations for people in which they can make connections to the feelings they have about what they're working on. If people work willingly with affirmations in this way, then things will come up. We don't need to do much more than that. All any of us need to do is to be willing to use an affirmation with some sort of persistence. Then these things can emerge and be let go of if that's appropriate.

Lastly, and perhaps the most important, is the idea that in using affirmations the words are a form of invocation. Words are immensely powerful and creative. The words written here can change your life forever. Things that have been said to me or that I have read have entered my psyche so deeply that I can see them as watersheds in my life when I look back.

Using an affirmation such as "I deserve a loving and supportive relationship" is an invocation to the universe that states that we are interested in and available for healthy intimacy. There may be resistance in us, but we are willing to face that and release it. We are then consciously and deliberately inviting the mysterious powers of the universe to assist in this adventure, as discussed in the last chapter. We are saying there is more in this than we know – that there is more in life than just our small selves. There is a certain humility in asking in this way. It's a form of prayer in which we acknowledge the limitations of the self and cultivate a readiness to face the unknown with courage. It's inviting and welcoming the power of the beyond.

▸ E X E R C I S E 8

Negative responses

This is an effective method for accessing and providing an outlet for your negative beliefs. Take a sheet of paper and draw a line down the middle. Write your affirmation on the left and immediately notice the first response or reaction that comes into your mind and write it down on the right side, as below. Repeat this at least ten times writing the same affirmation each time.

Affirmation	Response
I deserve the best.	No, you don't.
I deserve the best.	Rubbish!
I deserve the best.	You're not good enough.
I deserve the best.	Some hopes!
I deserve the best.	Maybe one day...
I deserve the best.	What is the best?
I deserve the best.	I don't have to earn it?
I deserve the best.	It sounds risky to me.
I deserve the best.	Are you sure?

Fill the page with both affirmation and responses. Your responses will show you what is in your subconscious mind in relation to the idea presented in the affirmation. Often the first answers are negative, but then they begin to change. You can see a process happening, as in the examples above. The answers often start off with outright rejection and then begin to be a little more open to the possibility. At some point you start to get positive answers. This change takes place at your pace. It may take days or weeks, depending on the individual, how much time and energy you are investing in your process of change, and also on how deeply your negative belief is held.

The information that appears in the right-hand column can be extremely helpful.

This exercise is a direct invitation to your subconscious to bring out what is hidden there. When you are sincere in your quest then your subconscious is often cooperative and reveals things that are buried in your memory. You can then bring these memories into the light of the present consciousness and ask yourself if they are still relevant. Plus you may wish to modify the original affirmation in the light of what the right-hand column reveals.

I recommend doing this at least twice a day for a week, focusing on one particular affirmation.

(For detailed instructions about the use of affirmations read Choose Your Thoughts, Change Your Life *by Jane Duncan. Details are at the back of the book.)*

He was unable to discriminate between "I'm feeling bad about something out there", and "I'm feeling bad in here."

CORE BELIEFS

We all have what I call core beliefs, beliefs which we remain largely unaware of. These can be ideas about ourselves, about the world, and about other people. For example, we all have ideas about our own feelings. Some people think that emotions are a kind of weakness. Others think emotions give them strength. Where do these ideas come from? By the time we are physically mature we hold many ideas that we formed on the basis of our experience. We also have many ideas that have been simply given to us and that we have accepted unquestioningly. Many of these ideas are unconscious. They are formed, or they begin to be formed, early in our lives. One way of seeing the work we do in healing ourselves is as bringing into awareness those unconscious beliefs which are no longer serving us.

An important part of this process is understanding that we regard as 'normal' whatever happens to us when we are growing up. While we're growing up, we generalise from those experiences; we see the world through them, and believe things about the world as a result of them. An example of this is what happened to children in Auschwitz during the war. They lived in a place surrounded by death, every day. After the war they were

taken to Israel to receive treatment from psychothera-
pists. They had to learn to change their fundamental
beliefs and perceptions of the world from death to life.
This is a very extreme example of how we generalise
from experiences, but it took these children a long time
and a lot of work before they began to be able to see life
in some measure as a positive, expansive possibility.

At the other end of the spectrum, there has been
research into what might be called functional, as
opposed to dysfunctional families – positive families.
Robin Skinner discusses this at length with John Cleese
in their book *Families and How to Survive Them*. This
research showed that members of these families, including the children, dealt with the events in life which are
considered to be stressful much more easily and quickly.
After a bereavement, for example, these families would
be through the process of bereavement so quickly that
people around them felt that they didn't care and that
they didn't show enough feeling or grief. If it were only
grief they expressed so briefly that might be fair criti-
cism, but when they moved house, members of these
families also made friends much more quickly than dysfunctional families. They'd be more likely to go out in
the garden and say to the neighbours "Hello, my name's
Fred", instead of staying in the house in some kind of
protective, defensive or isolated state, which would obvi-
ously not help them to form new relationships. It was
found that this outgoing effort helped these families to
deal with the stress of moving house.

In their family interactions, they were all much more
open with their feelings, sharing more. They had much
more interaction, and a better quality of it than less functional families. They clearly had a different set of beliefs

about themselves and their world.

A few years ago I met two children who impressed me incredibly strongly, because their experience was such a brutal and crude example of growing up in a dysfunctional family. An acquaintance was working as a foster mother and was looking after the two children, who had just been taken into care – they were a girl and a boy of about ten years old. I went to the house a couple of times while these children were there. They were extremely angry that they'd been taken away from their parents even though they had been beaten by them every day. This was normal to them. They felt they belonged in that environment and consequently they were extremely angry that they had been taken from their parents. These children had 'normalised' the experience of physical abuse.

Normalisation is part of the process of growing up for all of us. When we take in positive, supportive experiences as our norm then we are better equipped for love in our adult lives. It is our negative experiences that we need to address.

One of the ways in which negative experiences inform negative core beliefs is through a very simple mechanism that every young child has. When something is hurting them they are conceptually unable to do anything but take it personally and feel that they are to blame. One six-year old child I knew was talking to his mother about how unhappy he was because his father and mother were separated. He was experiencing pain over the separation, and it was emerging in nightmares. What he said to his mother was "If Daddy would come back and live here again, Mummy, I'll be good." He was experiencing pain at the absence of his father and at the distance between his parents, and felt that he could somehow affect it.

He was unable to discriminate between "I'm feeling bad about something out there", and "I'm feeling bad in here."

This is what happened to him (and to all of us in some form): something out there happens that's bad, and we feel pain or fear inside us. We are not able to make the distinction between "I am feeling bad about that out there", and "I am feeling bad in here". Which translates to: "It is me that is bad". When we are young there is a natural egotism in us that makes us see ourselves as the centre of the universe. So "There's something bad happening and I'm feeling bad" becomes "I am bad. There is something wrong with *me*" and in this case "If only I was good, Daddy would come back."

In this particular situation, these things emerged so they could be spoken about; he was able to be reassured by his mother and told "I understand that's how you're feeling, but your Daddy didn't leave because he doesn't like you, or because you've done anything bad." He may not want to take that in, but at least it's being said. I think in some sense he will take it in, and every child, I think, will listen to the parent or the adult there who's speaking in that loving way. And that's what children need, they need to have that distinction made for them because they are as yet unable to make it for themselves. They can only have it made for them by the parent. The child will have to take that on trust – but they take most things on trust at that age anyway, so I don't think that's particularly difficult.

When we have these forming experiences that become 'norming' experiences, we take them in and form beliefs about the world: about ourselves, others, love, relationships, work, men, women, relaxation, play, school, education, all these and more. With everything that we can think of that's important in our lives, our ideas about it have been formed, or at least begun to be formed, through our early experiences. We're not very sophisticated when these experiences start; this process begins early in our lives when we don't have the ability to discriminate and distinguish and when we are helpless and dependent.

A key core belief is ideally, *"I'm a good person, I am lovable."*

Other beliefs are like circles around that core. This central idea and the other beliefs around it are all formed within the context of the family. A family contains adults and maybe siblings, and other relatives, all living out their own beliefs largely unconsciously, until they become conscious of them.

It's hard to imagine a child growing up with very different beliefs from the people around them, because if they do differ in their beliefs, they will be in conflict with their parents and perhaps older siblings. We speak and act from our beliefs, and if they're different from other people's beliefs we are going to come into conflict with those people. Unless we are encouraged to develop our own ideas as a child, we are likely to go along with the dominant ideas because we are utterly dependent on these older people for every need – for food, shelter, love, warmth, for all our physical, emotional and spiritual needs. There's no more powerless relationship imaginable. A child is growing up for fifteen years – it is the longest period of dependence of any animal – and, until adolescence, most children will not go against the beliefs of those very powerful adults around them.

Imagine the helplessness of a child and its feelings, particularly if a parent is angry or disapproving or telling the child that it's in some way bad or naughty. The sense of helplessness in the face of our parents can be overwhelming even when we are grown-up, and this arises from the very straightforward reality of our recognition of how small we once were in relation to them.

I'd like to make a distinction between this and another kind of helplessness which relates to surrendering to God, or the Universe – the power that we invoke through prayer or affirmation we discussed in the last chapter. For any human, there are times when it is good to say "I don't know. I give in. I surrender. I'd like some help, I don't know what to do. Is there any point in doing anything?" Or, *"Perhaps I'd just better sit down, be quiet and listen."*

That's a positive helplessness. And there's a negative helplessness, based on our early core belief and experience of helplessness.

These core beliefs form a large part of our identity. "I am strong." "I am weak." "A man does this, not that." "A woman does this, not that." "I'm white, I'm black, I'm somewhere in between." These are all things about which we will have beliefs, about which we fix our identity. The more painful our early experiences, the more likely we are to be attached to our experiences and our identity, and the less likely we are, therefore, to want to change. It's a threat to our identity, a threat to who we think we are.

If a middle-class boy is in a working-class neighbourhood or vice versa, he's going to hang onto his middle-class identity and be different and suffer the consequences of that or he's going to give it up. If he gives it up, he's going to be a divided personality: a working-class boy at school, and a middle-class boy at home. He's going to grow up with a dual identity. Many people have a different voice in different company. It's interesting to enter with that person into different company and hear their voice change, hear them use a different vocabulary. We all have this ability, we're great actors, great deceivers and chameleon-like creatures.

Since we have these core beliefs and become identified with them, we also have an investment in that identity, and we don't want to change it. We want to hold on to these beliefs, not even knowing what they are most of the time. Because they come from the unconscious, they come out of the past, from forgotten experiences, so it's often a real challenge to know why we are behaving in the way that we do. Suddenly we are presented with a situation, perhaps stressful, and we behave in a particular way; something sort of pops out of us, and we haven't even known that's how we would be. Our behaviour in these moments is being informed by the past, it's not some sort of erratic or random behaviour, though it might seem like that. We have an identity, a set of ideas of who we are, that is more or less important to us to maintain. Our investment in staying true to our core beliefs, remaining identified with them, and in keeping things the same, is more if we have been hurt a lot, because there's a relationship between rigidity and pain. We are more likely to be rigid when we're in pain. We know that from our own physical experience. When we're in pain we stiffen. We become tense and find it hard to relax. And with emotional or spiritual pain, it's the same. The so-called functional families that I mentioned earlier don't have this difficulty, this rigidity, because they have experienced a more loving upbringing and therefore have less remembered pain in their unconscious. They are more flexible in their identifications and beliefs, they are more easy-going, it is easier for them to change their behaviour. This is an important part of the work of healing – loosening these ties that bind, these rigid parts of ourselves.

If we see that kind of rigidity, the first thing is to recognise that we're holding on, that we are rigidly identified. This has a message for us about the past, and we need to take some action. It's best not to go immediately into changing our beliefs but first to introduce some relaxation and acceptance of them and the underlying need for them in the past. Consciously trying to change them can come next, based on a firm foundation of self-acceptance.

We enter into all situations with a set of beliefs, through which we then interpret the world. I recently read an article in *Scientific American* (February 1996) by a scientist named Dennet. One experiment he created was to show people a series of flashing lights and ask them to indicate what the series was. He then imperceptibly speeded the series up and changed it. What he discovered was that people didn't see what was there, they saw what they thought was there. Once a simple pattern had been established, they saw that, and they continued to see it. But that wasn't what was there; when he slowed it down again, they could see that the pattern had changed. Their eyes were perfectly capable of seeing this all along – there was no problem about it visually; it was a question of interpretation. Dennet says we have a virtual reality machine inside our heads. I call this selective perception. Our beliefs inform our actual vision of the world, our interpretation of events.

A simple example: if somebody walks into the room and they don't smile, how do you interpret that? We all interpret something different, based on our past. It's amazing how powerful it is, just to have a straight face. People have all kinds of ideas about you if you have a straight face. It's the same with a smiling face: maybe we think that person's happy, or we think they like us. When we're aware of this, we begin to see daily examples of how selectively we perceive our reality. Given that we have that ability, we can go on confirming our beliefs.

This can be a real source of difficulties in intimate relationships. We need to know what are our unconscious assumptions about love and intimacy, about men and women, about sex and affection. When we are unaware what our assumptions are, we tend to interpret the world in the light of these assumptions without giving them any reality check.

For example, I slowly became aware that I interpreted my sexual partner saying "No" to making love with me as a personal rejection when it wasn't necessarily anything to do with me. Because I was subconsciously expecting rejection, when I heard "No", I felt rejected and hurt. With the benefit of hindsight, I can see that most of the time that was a misinterpretation based on negative beliefs that I was holding about myself and my sexuality.

We don't need to worry about our positive beliefs, unless they're leading us into false situations. There are aspects of us which are fine, and we don't need to do anything about them. Those functional families don't need to do much about changing negative patterns; they're doing all right the way they are. And they're in positive feedback too, so things are getting better. What we do need to do something about are the negative beliefs, the things that are pulling us down and restricting us and making us feel bad. The following exercise can reveal a great deal to you about your beliefs about yourself in a very short time.

▶ EXERCISE 9

Looking at our beliefs – "Tell me what I could say to you that would make you feel good/bad."

This is another partner exercise done in five minute sections. Decide who is A and who is B. A begins by saying "Tell me what I could say to you that would make you feel bad", and then relaxes into silence, into clean listening (see Exercise 2). B answers the question for five minutes by telling A anything that he or she can think of that would make them feel bad if A said it. Be aware what feelings emerge as you do this. The listener could make some brief notes so that what is said is not forgotten. After five minutes you change over and B asks and becomes the listener.

At the end of this second five minutes you both close your eyes and sit silently for a minute or two, feeling whatever is within you at that moment, and being aware of any thoughts or images.

Then A asks again changing the word 'bad' to 'good'. B then responds. After five minutes you change over.

Strangely, this version can often be more difficult – we are more used to our negative ideas about ourselves than to our positive ones.

Next, A helps B to look at some of the significant things that were said. Many of these will be negative core beliefs that B is holding. Even in the 'good' version you may be able to identify negative beliefs, e.g. "You can say that to me, and I like it; but that doesn't mean it's true."

B then does the same for A.

If you wish, you can then convert some of these negative beliefs into positive affirmations.

*Worrying is imagining
combined with fear.*

THE TYRANNY OF
THE IMAGINATION

As I mentioned before, on this path of personal growth we may be faced with many demons. It's a modern *Pilgrim's Progress*! These demons arise within us and are all angels in disguise, the shadows of angels. It's how we deal with them that matters, as they are tests of our understanding. Growth is not about being perfect, getting it right all the time. It's OK to make mistakes, some of which we may need to make over and over again until one day we get the message and stop.

There's one inner demon in particular that can be a real tyrant – and equally when we get out of its shadow, an angel. And that is the imagination.

Imagination is something we all have; it's a natural function of being human and being alive – perhaps we could say of being an animal. All animals have imagination, but as humans, I think we have it in very high degree, and it's a perfectly natural function of our minds. We can see this easily in children playing: they will be using their imagination in some form. They'll be making something up, creating something, building something, knocking something down; they'll even pretend to be somebody else.

This is a perfectly natural and delightful part of our being, but it can also become a tyranny when we're young. As children, we are playful in our minds, we're very free in how we're thinking, very magical in the way we think. (Joseph Chilton Pearce writes in great depth about these qualities of the child in his book *The Magical Child*; I recommend it.) These are very creative qualities, and one of the ways in which we use them as children is when we're in pain. When we're suffering for some reason or other, we use our imagination to escape.

Children can retreat very easily into a world of their own, which they create inside their minds using their imaginations.

I know this from my own experience. When I was growing up, the thing that really sustained me in difficult times was reading, which is a way of feeding the imagination, a way of having an imaginative experience. We read the words and enter into the story and live it in our minds.

I can remember one occasion when I was about ten years old. I went to the library during the summer holidays and got some books out – they were Biggles books, by Captain W. E. Johns. I thought they were great, really terrific! I took them home, I read them, and at about five o'clock that evening I went back to the library with those same four books ready to take out some more. I'd read them all that day, which was not unusual for me. The reason I remember this particular occasion was because the librarian wouldn't let me change them. It was against the rules; you couldn't exchange books that you'd taken out that day. I was very upset by this – because I wanted to continue reading. I didn't have anything to read and it was something I felt I needed desperately. Reading fulfilled a need for me and I felt bereft without a book as company.

When we're young, and suffering for whatever reason, we have this route of the imagination that we can take into our own inner world. It may be through books, it may be a fantasy world, through dolls, toys or guns, or whatever; but we have this route that we can take, and we all do it to a greater or lesser degree because it gives us a measure of comfort and control. We can remove ourselves from the immediate environment into our own imagined world.

This is the major way in which we tend to move out of our bodies and our feelings and into our minds. We have a tendency to go into our mental faculties, and one of the major mental faculties we have is imagination. What that means is that we live more in the imagination, more in the mind, than in our feelings and in our bodies, particularly if we are trying to avoid pain.

One of the most obvious qualities of the mind is that we can go anywhere in our imagination. Right now, we can go together to a tropical island.

Imagine a blue sea, and surf that's breaking on the reef; palm trees swaying, coconuts up in that tree, and the warmth of the sun on your body.

We can just go there, now. The body has to stay where it is but we can go out to this tropical island in our mind, using our imagination. If you went on a little fantasy journey just then, you will see just how easy this is for us to do.

Because we have this faculty to go anywhere using the imaginative aspect of the mind, when we're in pain as we're growing up, we will do that to escape the pain of our experience, which is in our bodies. So this is a natural defence mechanism that helps to carry us through difficult times and to escape feelings experienced in the body, in the belly maybe, or in the heart. You could say that we're driven from our bodies by painful experiences.

It doesn't have to happen that way, though. If something painful happens to you when you are small and there's a caring adult around you to support you, to hold you, to give you a hug, to hold your hand, to say "Yes, that hurts, doesn't it?" then you can be free of this need to go into imagination, and come down, come back into the body, and really feel the pain, cry and release it. Children do that very easily, if you can acknowledge what's happening to them in a caring way. They'll come into their bodies, they'll come into that feeling, and they'll cry or be angry. Whatever it is that they need to feel, that support will help them feel it. Without that support, there is a natural route out, and that is to go into the imagination. This is a wonderful faculty, a very powerful survival mechanism.

The hostage Brian Keenan, in his book *An Evil Cradling*, writes about being held in solitary confinement. He spends much of his time revisiting his past through his imagination and memory. He's under great stress: he is in fear for his life, he is beaten physically, he doesn't have enough room to move and exercise his body properly, he's kept there in very bad conditions, and he doesn't know how long he'll be there, so it's a very stressful situation. He survives by effectively leaving his body behind and going into his memory and his imagination.

It's a powerfully useful survival mechanism. The trouble is when it becomes a habit it's a tyranny and then our imagination drives our experience of life. For example, we worry. That is, we imagine something that *might* be going to happen, with anxiety. You never worry about something that is actually happening now – there's no need. When you're crossing the road, it's wise to be careful; but you don't need to worry if there's a car coming or not, you can see. It's there, it's present.

It's easy to have a habit of worrying, which is imagining combined with fear. This can be a very destructive pattern. In the same way that you can create an escape from fear, by imagining nice things, you can bring up fear by creating frightening images. By the time we're adults, we can be experts at using our imagination to make ourselves afraid. And we have a great deal of support for this. Turn on the radio, switch on the television, open a newspaper. The images that you see are images of fear and violence. They're images of negative experience. There's a newspaper called *Positive News* (details at the back of the book), which only has good news in it. It's been going for some years – it's a lovely newspaper, I recommend it – but compared to the mainstream media they don't sell very many copies. It's a truism in the media that good news doesn't sell papers. It would be nice to prove this wrong, but it seems that good news is not very interesting to people's imagination, because people are accustomed to imagining with fear. They're accustomed to imagining negative experience.

We need to be careful with our imaginings. Once we start to be aware that we have this ability it's like riding a lively horse; if you don't tell it where to go, it will go where it wants to go. It'll wander around, and may be very frisky. You may be riding alongside a hedge – suddenly there's a gap and the horse thinks it sees something move in there. It can jump off the ground and you can end up in the ditch. So if you're just sitting on the back of your horse, in this case your imagination, and you're letting it wander around, then anything can happen to you.

The other thing that the 'horse' may do is take you home – but it may not be the home you want to go to. It'll take you to the place where it feels safe. The place where our imagination feels safe is the past, or a reflection of the past. But our past experiences may not be nourishing to us now, in the present.

When I think of my imagination in this way, as a horse, then I realise I need to learn to ride it. I need to learn to encourage my imagination to go in the direction in which I want to go, not in the direction of my habits from the past.

We begin to do this by first being conscious of how we are using our imagination. When we have some awareness of it, then we can do something about it.

If we start to be conscious of this faculty of imagination – which could be tyrannising our lives because we're not taking charge of it, and creating feelings in us that we don't need any more – then we can begin to take charge of this faculty, to turn it around and make it go in the direction we want it to go. But like learning to ride a horse, that might take a little time. It is not so easy to do straight away, but we can start to take it in hand, we can start to learn to 'ride' it, we can start to have it go in the direction we choose. We have a choice about where we're going.

One of the worst imaginative tyrannies that we have to face is to do with love and sex. These days we are bombarded with images of sex and love, which stimulate our imaginations. If we are imagining sex or love whilst with a sexual partner, then we are not fully present with them, because we are not fully present in our bodies. If we are not present in our bodies, then our capacity for closeness and intimacy diminishes.

If we're engaging in a sexual act and imagining something, we're not present in the way that we could be if we're not imagining. We're removed in some measure – a large measure, in my opinion. We are absent. It's the same with love. If we imagine we're in love with somebody, we're not in love with them, we're in our imagination.

We are full of imagined notions about sex and love. We've been exposed to these images over and over and over, and they're very seductive. If as children we learnt to withdraw from the body into the mind and the imagination to escape from suffering pain, as adults we use this faculty to comfort ourselves by imagining love in all its forms, including sex.

For example, reading about love, about romance, can be a comfort; or going to the movies, where the stars go through the dance of falling in love and at the end come together, makes us feel really good. Wasn't that a lovely movie? There's nothing wrong with this – unless we are using reading or movies as a substitute for a direct experience of love. When we start to be aware of how much these fantasies are taking us away, then we start to confront how much we don't want to be here in the present. How much we don't actually want to be in this moment, now, here, in this body, being with whatever we might feel.

If you meditate, you'll know the experience of trying to be in the present, and how the mind and the imagination carry us off; most people aren't able to sit even for one minute without going off on some train of thought.

But once we start to realise that this is what's happening, we can start to control it. It's in our hands. It's in our minds, our imaginations, our thoughts. I'm not saying it's easy to do this, but the fact is, if we don't do it, our imagination will wander about at its own will, which is based on past, early experience and the need to defend ourselves. Our imagination will tend to take us back to the safe places where we're removed from our feelings. We either go back there, back to that stable with the horse, or we go where we want to go. Which, of course, means that we have to start thinking about where we want to go.

I want to suggest to you an affirmation which says:

I use my imagination to help me go where I want to in my life.

If you put that up on your bathroom mirror or some other place where you will see it every morning, it could have a great impact on your thoughts, and in your life.

There's no harm in the horse of our imagination; in fact, there's a lot of good in it, as long as we are riding it and not the other way round.

Beautiful gifts, precious, wonderful gifts, come to us if we are open and take charge.

▶ EXERCISE 10

The light visualisation exercise

This is a visualisation that uses the image of light. The light can symbolise whatever you wish. It can be a way of relaxing, or a healing light; a way of connecting with the spirit, or anything you choose.

Find a comfortable place where you will be undisturbed for a few minutes. Do it at your own pace. Either lying down or sitting, take a few deep breaths and begin to relax. In your mind's eye imagine a column of white light above your head then imagine this light entering gently into your body through the crown of your head. Let your jaw be relaxed, and let the light begin to soothe away any tension you are feeling. Let the light move down into your neck and shoulders easing away any tension.

As you breathe in, imagine breathing in more light. As you breathe out, release any tension. Feel the light gently move down your arms and out of your fingers, back into the universe.

Now your chest; let the light move slowly down through the upper part of your body, down your spine, calming and easing your whole back. Take your time over this.

Let the light move into your stomach, easing your digestive system, and then down into the pelvis and genitals, down through your legs and out of your feet.

Now connect the whole of your body from the top of your head to your toes, breathing in the light and out again. Allow yourself to be supported and cherished by this stream of light.

Let yourself be relaxed in this state for as long as you wish and then slowly return to a fully alert state, reminding yourself of your body by wiggling your fingers and toes, and taking a few deep breaths, and move gently towards opening your eyes and coming back to your surroundings.

(This is adapted from The White Light Meditation *on the audiotape* Life Supports You *by Jane Duncan. Details are at the back of the book.)*

*It appears that commitment means
losing freedom, particularly
to the male.*

FREEDOM AND COMMITMENT

I think that men traditionally, and perhaps even biologically, have a greater interest in freedom than in commitment. For women, I think it's the other way round. Of course, we all have male and female characteristics inside us and we don't need to conform to gender stereotypes. However, if we look around us, we can see that women are generally more interested in relating, while men are more interested in sex. You don't see many women buying porn magazines, just as you don't see many men reading Barbara Cartland novels, and there are millions of both of these sold. There are reasons for this and one is that sex doesn't require relationship or commitment. It doesn't require continuity. Relationship does.

It appears that commitment means losing freedom, particularly to the male. It is even defined in the *Oxford English Dictionary* as "Engagement that restricts freedom of action".

There is an archetype with which we are all very familiar that represents this, and that is the cowboy, the high plains drifter. He is the man in the movies who can handle being single, who drifts into town on horseback,

drifts back out again and never forms a relationship. He
has no commitment, he doesn't engage with people, or
even very much with the world. There is a song called
'Desperado' by the American group 'The Eagles' which
sums up this image incredibly well. The lyrics urge the
rider to come to his senses, and telling him that he's been
out riding fences too long.

It's such a good image of the cowboy out there riding
the range, riding the fences, and the double meaning is
beautiful. He's been sitting on the fence, he doesn't want
to come down off it and engage with somebody, and he
doesn't want to be in his senses either. He wants to avoid
his senses; the last thing he wants to do is feel something.
He's tough, he can handle it. He'll be out in the cold and
the snow, in the heat and the sunshine and he'll just put
his hat on and be fine.

The song points out that the things that have been
pleasing him can also hurt him, in that the loneliness
which freedom can bring is not nourishing. He may have
had a long period in his life where he has enjoyed the
freedom of drifting around, but in the end he's going to
be hurt by it if he doesn't come down off the fence and
start to engage with others. To him freedom is empty
and he's trapped in it as though he's in a prison. If he
can't make a relationship, he *is* in a prison of loneliness,
where he knows nothing about commitment or relationships, and freedom *is* empty, just a word.

The next lines are about him losing all his highs and
lows, and losing his capacity to feel. When we are young
and uncommitted, less mature, we do get these highs
and lows. There is wonderful drama in our lives, but as
we get a little more mature, a little bit older, we start to
lose both the highs and lows, and then things may start

to feel a bit empty. What life is saying then, in my understanding, is "What about commitment?"

The final line of the song urges the cowboy to let somebody love him, to get off the fence and open the gate before it's too late. "Open the gate" means opening the gate into himself and into his heart – opening to another person. You can't have the amazing freedom that exists within an intimate relationship without commitment. As I already said, it is in the garden of truth that love grows and it is commitment that defines these boundaries. Inside there we can expand and explore the vulnerabilities of intimacy in an atmosphere of truthfulness and developing trust. Within these boundaries we can leave the more superficial aspects of our personalities, our interest in how things look, for example, and go deeper into the way things feel from within ourselves. It is in this garden that we can develop the freedom to love and be loved, to be seen as we are and accept the other as they are.

I think this song is a powerful image for men in our culture. I'm sure that some women have the same issues with commitment, but maybe they have them in somewhat different forms. Generally, women have had much more straightforward conditioning about relationships and commitment.

One of the traps people get caught in is thinking they are looking for a relationship but then finding themselves repeatedly in relationships with men or women who don't want a relationship. This looks like wanting a relationship, but if you look back on your life, you may realise that there have been a whole series of people you were with who didn't want a relationship. Then I think you have to acknowledge what has happened with all these partners and see the common theme, which is that they didn't want a relationship. In the end you realise that it is your issue; it is actually you who doesn't want relationship, it's you who is afraid of commitment and intimacy. It is you that is afraid of being connected, with all the risks involved in commitment.

So here we have an image of freedom, which I would say is immature, that is adolescent and youthful – it has its beauty, it has its place – but it's not something that is ultimately going to bring you satisfaction. It will be unfulfilling in the long run.

It's a kind of freedom that says "I can do what I want, I can go where I like. I don't answer to anybody." It's rebellious. It's saying "I've had enough of being told what to do by my parents and my teachers, all these people. I'm going to do what I want to do." And so the Desperado rides off, and he (or she) goes where he wants to, sleeps where he wants.

One of the most common negative images of commitment is that it is something you can't get out of. For example, many people still think that if you get married you shouldn't be able to get divorced without blaming somebody. Before the Second World War, people who got married had to stay married, or risk facing the most terrible condemnation by the society around them. So here we have an image of commitment – in this example, marriage – which has been made negative in our minds, because it can be a terrible burden if there is no way out. I'm not advocating that people get married casually just because it is easy to get divorced. What I'm saying is that I think we have been led to fear that if we do commit ourselves we are somehow imprisoned by that commitment.

The paradox is that commitment without freedom is not healthy.

If you enter into or remain in a partnership with anybody under duress, whether it's a marriage or a business partnership, then that's not a healthy relationship. That's not going to lead you, or the other person, in a positive direction in life. Often people meet and they think they are going to love each other for ever, so they decide to get married. That's all freely done and they make a commitment and then, perhaps, after a while they find that things are not quite as easy as they looked. If those people stay in the relationship just because they made a promise it's not likely to be a very happy experience. It takes a lot more than a promise to make a relationship develop. I'm not knocking marriage or other rituals, it's very helpful to make vows especially before our friends and families, but this is only the beginning.

More than ever before, if we stay in a marriage it needs to be because we choose to do so. We do not need to remain married because we said we would ten years ago. Our commitment needs to be remade each day. It is very helpful to recognise that we are choosing daily. Whatever relationship we are committing to, we are choosing to be committed to that relationship. If we choose not to, we don't ever have to speak to that person again in our lives – mother, father, husband, wife, sister, brother. It doesn't matter who it is, that's our choice. We can pretend that it's not our choice, but it is. Of course, we have to be willing to take the consequences; but we're getting some consequences anyway, aren't we?

We often pretend to ourselves we're not choosing, that we're victims of terrible circumstances. This self-deception is a re-enactment of being a child, when we didn't have the choices that we have as adults. If we pretend that we don't have this freedom we can get into some very unpleasant places inside where we feel stuck and trapped, for example, where we feel we are a victim of the other person's moods. But in intimate relationship no adult is a victim. You can say to that person whatever you need to say to them, for example, *"I'm not here to be the target of your bad moods. If I can help in any way I am willing to do that; but I am not willing to be a scapegoat!"*

If we are playing the game of "I'm not free", it makes it much more difficult to make these statements.

If we're in a relationship with someone who doesn't want to be committed we are not in a committed relationship, because commitment takes two people. We can be in a relationship with someone who is running around all over the place, but what kind of commitment is that?

I think women often have a tendency to compromise in relationships, letting men get away with stuff and then feeling quietly superior. This to me is a symptom of not feeling free, because when we feel free in our relationships, we confront this kind of thing. We don't put up with behaviour we don't like and we stop making allowances for other people if it's not in the best interests of the relationship. At its most extreme there is a danger of infantilisation, of making the man into a child and the woman into some kind of maternal figure. She is then taking care of him and at the same time resenting him. Who wants to be acting like a mother all her life?

There are also times when the opposite roles are evident, where the husband is father, the man of the house, and the woman doesn't know how to do things and he takes care of her financially. He's out in the world and she's in the home. She's behaving like a child: she doesn't know how to do deal with money and the car, and he's behaving like a father. It's just as destructive.

This attitude contributes to all kinds of resentments and feelings of being stuck. If we feel free we won't do this, we will be tougher. We will be straight and say "No this is not OK for me. I'm not accepting this in this relationship. This is what I want. I want the best for me and the best for you too."

This to me is what commitment is about. If I'm committed to a relationship, I'm committed to having the best. Not making the best of it, which can be a compromise, but having the best. If we are going to be committed to something, let's be committed to the highest in ourselves, in our relationships, in our lives.

The commitment that I am advocating is first and foremost a commitment to truth. With this as a foundation we can build a positive relationship with confidence. We can look for healthy love and intimacy. This kind of commitment provides the right environment for the development of love and is a commitment to the idea that we deserve love. I see commitment as the boundaries of a garden; how big it is and what's in the garden is a matter of personal choice. Within this special area we plant truth and encourage it to grow, and the flowers are love.

We make a choice to love. We can make a marriage vow "Till death us do part" because it comes from the heart and not the head, and the heart doesn't make distinctions about time. The heart is willing to be fully committed and to face the unknown.

So freedom and commitment are not in any way opposites, rather they are complementary, completely linked and part of each other. The freedom to wander around the world lonely is a very empty freedom. The freedom that exists within committed relationships is immense and doesn't need to be understood, because there are no guarantees in life, no matter how hard we try to make things look that way. To enter into committed relationship, we need to have courage (the courage of the heart). We need to be able to risk, to be able to say, "OK, I'm going to go for it". And that means every day, not just when we stand in front of the congregation in a marriage ceremony. It means every day we are committed and we choose this commitment. If we pretend that we are trapped in this commitment, then we will suffer and so will our partner. Then comes the opportunity for the partner to say "Wake up, you are acting as if you are trapped. Not true – wake up – it's not true." And once again, we find ourselves in a place where we can remake our choice to be committed.

► EXERCISE 11

The unconditional favour

This is a risky exercise!

Make an agreement with your partner (or someone else you are close to) to exchange unconditional favours. By this you agree to do *whatever* is asked (without previous knowledge) as long as it is not against the law, nor something that would be destructive to yourself or others. To begin with you can make it less risky by creating some agreed prior conditions. It is also good to put some time boundaries on it, say ten minutes to start with.

This exercise is about having fun and experiencing the fact that agreeing to the other person's requests can be enjoyable.

*Sex in the environment of truth
is lovemaking.*

SEX AND PLEASURE

If you are willing to follow the ideas put forward in the earlier chapters then you are willing to be open and vulnerable (when appropriate). When we bring these qualities to sex we create a very powerful opportunity to enjoy ourselves in what I believe is the real purpose of sex, beyond the obvious biological need for procreation. This purpose is to help us to stay together. The pleasure we receive through open and vulnerable lovemaking is a bonding device that nature has provided to help us through the difficult times in our relationships. (Desmond Morris in *The Naked Ape* discusses this from a biological viewpoint and suggests that there is no other obvious reason for our eroticism than to reinforce the pair-bond. He also gives a technical description of making love that is extremely funny.)

Lovemaking is therefore different from sex and much more interesting and enjoyable; sex in the environment of truth *is* lovemaking. It is not about power or control or domination. It is about an extraordinary ability that exists within our bodies to feel pleasure. We can repeat the same movements and experience the same or very similar sensations time after time with the same person without tiring of them. This is a miracle of love, for which we can be profoundly grateful.

Because we are being truthful (as best we can) we do not have to be sexual performers or athletes. Our first concern is authenticity, not the insecurity of playing a role to bolster some image of ourselves in our own or another's eyes. Nor do we need the sexual hype of adultery and all the excitement of forbidden fruit that is all around us in the media these days.

A good example of this forbidden fruit excitement is the recent film *The English Patient,* which won so many awards. It's a gorgeous film – full of sensual, visual images that delighted my eyes. There is one moment when the camera pans across the patient's bed and as he reminisces, the folds of the blanket magically become the rumpled surface of the desert dunes seen from a plane. It deserves its awards; but there's one thing I disliked – the drama of the infidelity. This beautiful film and its moving story lend glamour to infidelity and so validate it. Why are we so attracted to this particular drama? Whatever it is, I find myself more and more objecting to the dishonesty of adultery in the films and plays I see.

This particular film has great characters, wonderfully dramatic desert scenery, the excitement of discovery, handsome men, beautiful women, the danger and intrigue of war and the resulting conflicts of loyalty. Do we really need the added zest of illicit sex and so-called love?

I am willing to acknowledge the passion of the two lovers, their intensity and the beauty of their absorption. But is this love? My answer is, no, it isn't. They fall in my estimation because they become liars. They have no respect for truth. Their tragedy is devalued because they prefer the drama of their infidelity to facing up to the fact that their need and desire is not only for each other but also a desire and a need for something secret. Why do such affairs have to be concealed from the eyes of, in this case, the husband and their friends and society? Their sexual passion is heightened by the added spice of shame and guilt. They are like teenagers in a steamed-up phone box: the forbidden fruit tastes so much juicier than the tamer fare of honest and open relationship.

Would they still be so 'in love' (I prefer 'obsessed'), if they went to her husband and told him the truth? Would their love survive being open instead of secret? We'll never know. Would her bleak, dark death be different if their love was not so hidden? Would his grief as he fulfils his promise and carries her from her tomb be less? Would our perceptions change if the plot did not have this adulterous element? I don't think so. Her awful, lonely death and his futile battle to save her transcend their history and elevate both characters to heroic proportions. Their true tragedy is demeaned by their lies.

This is a glorification of lies and infidelity. Lies and infidelity are not glorious, they are sordid. Love flourishes in truth, not in deceit. This may make our lives difficult sometimes but this is also how we learn and grow. It is not manly to make love with another man's wife and then sit down to dinner with him. It's dishonest and puerile. It's not womanly to lie and cheat the man you have exchanged vows with, it's adolescent and based in fear. If you feel good about yourself and what you are doing, do you need to lie? It takes courage to be truthful and there's plenty of drama in it, too, just like the film, which is full of images of courage.

If you feel that sex is not interesting enough, then instead of looking outside yourself, or outside your relationships for excitement, look inside. If you apply the ideas in this book you will find that you can take charge of your sex life in a new way. Doing this with your partner you will both be demonstrating love and commitment, and actively, consciously, creating a firm foundation for your relationship.

Consciously choose to be in your body while lovemaking.While touching each other's bodies all over, stay with the sensations you feel, rather than rushing to touch the genitals and/or breasts. The quality of sensation in your body depends to a large extent on your ability to give attention to it. You may experience pleasure in many parts of your body that will suprise you if you do this. Many people will need to rein in their imagination (see chapter ten) in order to do this. If this is true for you, persist with it and you will be rewarded. The sexual excitement you get from being deeper in your body is quite different from what you feel when you are not fully in the sensations.

Be willing and ready to stop. Making love can be a delicate and vulnerable experience. It can bring up fear; old memories can emerge; past pain or anger may suddenly interfere, and it's good to stop when this happens. If you don't stop, you have to repress these emotions again, and energy will be lost in doing that, energy that could be contributing to your enjoyment. You will also miss an opportunity for understanding that could be liberating.

One of you may want to stop for no obvious reason at all and this is very important to respect. It's not loving to make love if one of you doesn't feel like it. It can be scary to stop and start like this, but if you keep in touch with each other and keep communicating, you will be developing truthfulness between you.

Be honest with yourself and your partner. Talk about sex and what you enjoy and also any dissatisfactions. The clean listening exercise in chapter two can be very helpful in providing a space and time for you to speak of things that may be difficult or unclear. Being inhibited in talking about sex is something that needs to be challenged in intimate sexual relationships. It is a loving act to want to know how your partner is feeling. Don't be fobbed off or put off by their reluctance.

Going within yourself (see chapter five) helps you to know more of what turns you on. You will also be able to express your pleasure more because you are more in touch with what's inside you. The wonderful interplay between giving and receiving pleasure is deepened by this. The more you know, the more you can share and therefore the more you bring to your partner in every moment, especially in the deep closeness of lovemaking.

Taking care to be truthful brings us many rewards. If we are having difficulty finding pleasure in our lovemaking, we don't need to find an illicit lover. We need to return to the basics outlined in chapter one and ask "Do you feel loved by me?" After exploring this and finding out where we both are and what works and doesn't work, the next level is to find out what feelings are unexpressed which may be in the way. This could be anger, fear, pain and even love itself. Keep out all the fantasies and imaginings, and look for pleasure; enjoy the pleasure of lovemaking in the clear atmosphere of truth and the wonderful quality of being in the present.

▶ EXERCISE 12

Touching all over

Set aside forty minutes and be together in your bedroom, making sure it's warm enough. Choose some quiet, relaxing music to play in the background and, if you both want it, have a massage oil to use. There are oils with beautiful, sensual aromas.

Decide who will give first and who will receive. You will have fifteen minutes each.

The receiver lies naked on the bed. The active partner is going to stroke them gently all over their body, but not the genitals or breasts. It is not intended to be a direct erotic arousal, though this may happen. If arousal does happen, don't pursue that at this time, stay with simple stroking. Keep bringing your attention to your bodily sensations from within yourself and limit any expression to small movements or signals. Choose the idea that this is a special time for you to relax and go inside with no demands for you to give anything at all. It is a time just to receive.

After fourteen minutes the giver starts to bring it gently to a close and then after a minute or two of quiet, change over.

Equally, when you are giving, take the opportunity to be fully in the simple act of touching this body before you, let your hands move slowly and softly and enjoy the sensations that you are feeling through your hands.

Spend a few minutes telling each other how it was for you in both roles.

AFTERWORD

In the beginning of this book I wrote:

"I deserve a loving and supportive relationship."

This is true for all of us.

In our mind's eye we can place this on a large banner ten feet wide and hang it on the wall. We can let it hang there always as a reminder of what is possible.

We deserve loving and supportive relationships because we were born. We don't need to do anything else to deserve them. Looking at a baby, you'll know what I'm talking about. This infant does not need to do anything, does not need to say anything, does not need to be anything, other than be alive in its body, in order to deserve love and support. And we've all got a body. We were all that infant, every one of us, and that infant will always be part of us until we stop breathing.

We think we've got to earn it. That's not true. The idea that we've got to earn it, to do something to deserve it, is something that we've been given through our experience of life, and it's a mistaken notion. It can be difficult to get rid of, but the fact that it wants to stay with us doesn't make it any less mistaken.

We deserve love simply because we exist. What we can do is allow the truth of this to encourage us to bring it more fully alive in our lives right now.

RESOURCES

Living Well is owned and run by Philip Rogers and Jane Duncan. Both trained counsellors, they offer individual sessions, run groups and workshops, and give talks.

WORKSHOPS
Please call 07050 074875 for up-to-date information.

AUDIOTAPES
(see following pages)

ON COMPACT DISC
TRUTH IN THE PROCESS OF CHANGE
A live talk by Philip Rogers with questions and answers

POSITIVE NEWS
A quarterly newspaper available on subscription. Call 01588 630121.

To order any of our books and tapes or the CD, please contact us at the address below.

Living Well, PO Box 980, Oxford OX2 0YB
Tel: 07050 074875

BOOKS

Recommended by Louise L. Hay, this is an invaluable guide to how to use affirmations so that they really work. Too often we buy into the negative thoughts we have in response to a positive idea; Jane explains why this happens and helps you connect with more of what you actually want out of life. A life-changing book in more ways than one.

(Jane also offers a correspondence course based on the book.)

We offer a few selected titles that we recommend, for example, *The Prophet* or *The Creative Companion*. Please call for up-to-date information.

TAPES

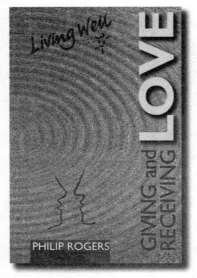

This is the tape that goes with Exercise 1 on page 16. It is designed to give you an experience of the powerful effect of consciously choosing to love and be loved. It guides you and a partner through a process of giving and receiving love, without physical contact, and encourages you to experience the intimacy this can bring. After a while, using the music alone will help to engender this feeling.

SIDE 1   Explains what to do, step by step, beginning with one minute for each person giving and receiving and building up to longer periods.

SIDE 2   The background music for you to use at other times to enhance intimacy as and when you choose.

        Length: approx 50 minutes

        Music by Brian Boothby

TAPES

This is the tape that goes with Exercise 5 on page 60.

SIDE 1   Philip talks you gently through a process of becoming aware of your breath and some of the difficulties that you might meet while doing this. The breath is the giver of life and learning to explore your inner world in this way is a simple and practical route into meditation.

SIDE 2   Twenty minutes of silence signalled for you at the beginning and end with the sound of a Tibetan gong, with a brief introduction and invocation.

Length: approx 45 minutes

TAPES

Use this tape to help you relax...

◆ On waking
◆ On going to sleep
◆ Travelling to work
◆ During breaks or lunch hours
◆ Any time you feel you need a breather

Listening to Philip's calm and soothing voice, you are encouraged to simply take five minutes to relax your mind and body. No need to set aside half an hour any more – this tape can be used at any point during your day (except while driving) to help you release stress and invite calmness and peace of mind.

Length: 6 minutes, same each side

TAPES

Affirmations are positive statements that help you to change your beliefs about yourself and your world.

SIDE 1   Jane talks about the thinking behind the use of affirmations and how we can change our lives by catching our thoughts.

SIDE 2   Affirmations set to music on life, the body, health, love and intimacy, relationships, creativity, letting go/forgiveness and feelings.

Length: approx 60 minutes

TAPES

This is the tape that goes with Exercise 10 on page 116.

SIDE 1   White Light Meditation. Use light as a support, to help you feel safe, to feel that you belong and to feel calmer.

SIDE 2   Taking off your armour. Develop more satisfying relationships and begin to feel better about yourself by learning about your protective armour.

Length: approx 40 minutes

Music by Brian Boothby

TAPES

Powerful affirmations covering self esteem in all areas, including the body and feelings, relationships and love, and creativity and work.

Listening to this tape, and using the space in between the affirmations to repeat them to yourself, will help you change any negative beliefs you have to more positive and supportive ones. It is likely that at first you will not believe the positive affirmations; this is because you actually believe the opposite. So don't worry if you find yourself thinking that's not true, or something similar – as time goes on, and you continue repeating the affirmations, you will find your responses to them changing.

Length: approx 55 minutes

Music by Brian Boothby

ABOUT THE AUTHOR

Born in 1945, Philip Rogers has three adult children from a previous marriage, and three grandchildren. After the break-up of his first marriage he became deeply interested in psychology and meditation. During that time, he re-trained as a carpenter and supported himself as a builder and cabinet-maker over the next fifteen years while searching for answers to some of life's perennial questions "Who am I?" "What am I here for?" "How do I find love?" "Why is life the way it is?" "Where can I find all this out?"

In 1973 he travelled to India and joined a spiritual community to learn about meditation. After seven years in India, he continued his search in Europe and America, teaching meditation and practising as a personal development trainer. All this contributed to his ideas about the links between psychotherapy, meditation and relaxation.

At the end of the Eighties after a serious illness, he returned to the UK and began his private psychotherapy practice, running workshops and seeing couples and individual clients. He is a member of the Association of Humanistic Psychology Practitioners. He now lives in Oxford, running Living Well with his wife, Jane Duncan. He is also a director and partner in two counselling organisations.

He says "I see life as a journey towards understanding ourselves. What has helped me most on that path has been the mirror of my relationships."